Estate Planning Essentials

A Comprehensive Guide to Preserving Your Estate, Minimizing Probate, and Ensuring Your Legacy

Jeff Kikel ChFC, CRPC, CCFS

CPTX Media LLC

Copyright © 2024 by Jeff Kikel

Published by CPTX Media, LLC, Cedar Park, Texas 78613

All rights reserved. No portion of this book may be reproduced, stored in a retrieval system, or transmitted in any form or by any means – electronic, mechanical, photocopy, recording, scanning, or other – except for brief quotations in critical reviews or articles, without the prior written permission of the publisher.

The publication is designed to provide accurate and authoritative information with regard to the subject matter covered. It is sold with the understanding that the publisher is not engaged in rendering financial, accounting, or other professional advice. If financial advice or other expertise is required, the services of a competent professional should be sought.

If you are interested in bulk orders of this book or any of the series, please feel free to reach out to Jeff.Kikel@CPTXMedia.com

Contents

A Gift For You Before We Start	1
1. Introduction: Why Estate Planning is Essential	3
2. Understanding the Foundation of Estate Planning	9
3. The Essential Documents You Need	17
4. Debunking Common Misconceptions About Estate Planning	25
5. How to Avoid Probate	33
6. Planning for Healthcare and Incapacity	43
7. Family Dynamics and Communication	53
Make a Difference with Your Review	61
8. Creating a Will That Reflects Your Wishes	65
9. Exploring Trusts and Their Benefits	73
10. Addressing Digital Assets and Modern Challenges	81
11. Minimizing Taxes Through Strategic Estate Planning	89
12. Navigating Family Dynamics in Blended Families	97
13. Regularly Reviewing and Updating Your Plan	107

14. Legacy Planning—Building Meaning That Lasts	117
15. Ensuring Peace of Mind Through Comprehensive Planning	125
16. Conclusion: Taking the First Step	133
Keeping the Legacy Alive	137
Glossary	141
Index	147
Other Books By Jeff Kikel	153
About The Author	157

A Gift For You Before We Start

One of the key things that makes Estate Planning work in the long run is organization. With that in mind, I have created a resource page on our website that includes several worksheets and guides I have created or borrowed from our Estate Planning partner, Trust & Will. Those are free for you to use, and I hope they help you organize things as you go through this journey.

The resource page links to our friends at Trust & Will. The link entitles you to 10% off their already low-cost Estate Planning Solution. We receive no compensation from Trust & Will, and the 10%

discount is the same as my Estate Planning clients receive, so this is a completely unbiased recommendation. Their process is easy and thorough.

Please scan the QR code to go to the review site or click on the link below:

https://www.surehorizonretirement.com/estate-planning-essentials

Chapter One

Introduction: Why Estate Planning is Essential

Let me start by asking: Have you ever heard about Prince, the legendary musician, and his estate planning fiasco? You'd think someone with that much money would have a rock-solid plan in place, right? Wrong. When Prince passed away, he didn't leave a will. The result? Years of courtroom drama, family fights, and a lot of money lost to legal fees and taxes. The moral of the story: It doesn't matter how much—or how little—you have; if you don't have an estate plan, someone else decides what happens to everything you leave behind.

You might think, "Well, I'm not a celebrity or a millionaire. Do I really need to think about estate planning?" The answer is an enthusiastic yes! Estate planning isn't just for the rich and famous—it's for anyone who wants to make life a little easier for their loved ones when they're gone. It's about making sure your wishes are respected, avoiding unnecessary stress for your family, and, yes, even saving a little money in the process. Imagine the relief you could bring to your family by sparing them the stress and emotional burden of dealing with your affairs without a plan in place.

But let's be honest: the term "estate planning" can feel intimidating. It sounds like something reserved for lawyers and accountants, not everyday folks like you and me. You might picture piles of paperwork, complicated legal terms, and a hefty price tag. I get it. That's why this book exists—to break things down in plain English and show you that estate planning doesn't have to be overwhelming. In fact, it can be simple, empowering, and, dare I say, even enjoyable (okay, that last one might be a stretch, but we'll try). With the right guidance, you can navigate the process with confidence and a sense of control.

What is Estate Planning, Really?

At its core, estate planning is about answering one big question: What happens to my stuff when I'm gone? That's it. "Stuff" can mean your house, savings account, favorite fishing rod, or even family recipes. It's everything you've worked for, big or small.

But estate planning is also about more than just dividing your things. It's about making decisions that reflect your values. Who should take care of your kids if you're no longer around? What kind of medical treatment would you want if you couldn't speak for yourself? And how can you make sure your family avoids fighting over who gets Grandpa's vintage record collection? These are the kinds of questions estate planning helps you answer.

Why People Avoid Estate Planning

Let's talk about why most people procrastinate when it comes to estate planning. Here are the top three excuses I've heard:

1. **"I don't have enough to worry about."** Estate planning is about something other than the size of your bank account. Even if you don't think you have much, chances are you own something meaningful. A car, a small savings account, or maybe even a pet. It all matters.

2. **"It's too expensive."** Sure, hiring a fancy estate attorney can cost a lot, but there are plenty of affordable options. Plus, the cost of NOT planning—think court fees, legal battles, and taxes—can be far worse.

3. **"I don't want to think about dying."** I get it—nobody likes to think about their own mortality. But here's the thing: estate planning isn't about death. It's about life—your life, your loved ones' lives, and the legacy you'll leave behind.

What This Book Will Do for You

This book isn't going to bury you in legal mumbo jumbo or bore you with tax codes. Instead, we will have an honest, straightforward chat about what estate planning is, why it matters, and how you can do it without pulling your hair out.

Here's what you can expect:

- **Clarity:** We'll break down confusing topics like wills, trusts, and probate into bite-sized pieces you can actually understand.

- **Actionable Steps:** Each chapter will end with simple tasks you can tackle right away, so you'll feel like you're making progress.

- **Stories:** From celebrities to everyday folks, I'll share real-life examples of what can go wrong without a plan—and how you can avoid the same mistakes.

- **Peace of Mind:** By the time you finish this book, you'll understand how to protect what matters most to you.

Estate Planning is for Everyone

You don't need to be wealthy or have a sprawling estate to benefit from a bit of planning. Whether you're a single parent trying to make sure your kids are taken care of, a retiree looking to pass down a family heirloom, or just someone who wants to make life easier for their loved ones, estate planning is for you. Your unique circumstances and needs are at the heart of this process, and we're here to help you navigate them.

Let me share a quick story. A friend of mine, let's call her Linda, didn't think she needed a will. "I don't have much," she'd say. But when she passed unexpectedly, her kids spent months sorting through her finances and trying to figure out what to do with her house. It was stressful, expensive, and emotionally draining. If Linda had spent just a couple of hours creating a simple will, all of that could have been avoided.

Let's Get Started

You don't need to tackle everything at once. Estate planning is a process, not a one-time task. Think of it as building a safety net for your loved ones—one small step at a time. And here's the good news: you've already taken the first step just by picking up this book.

So grab a cup of coffee, find a comfy chair, and let's dive in. By the end of this journey, you'll not only understand estate planning—you'll own it. And trust me, your future self (and your family) will thank you.

Now, let's get started!

Chapter Two

Understanding the Foundation of Estate Planning

Let me tell you about Tom and Susan. They were your typical couple—married for 35 years, with two grown kids, a cozy home, and a small nest egg. Tom worked hard as a contractor, and Susan was a schoolteacher who loved gardening on the weekends. They didn't consider themselves wealthy, but they had a life they were proud of. They thought estate planning was something for "other people"—you know, the rich ones with mansions and trust funds.

When Tom passed away after an accident at work, everything changed. He didn't have a will, and Susan assumed their modest life meant settling his affairs would be simple. But that wasn't the case. With no estate plan in place, Susan found herself knee-deep in paperwork and legal battles. The house was in Tom's name as was his Brokerage account that he had inherited from his parents where most of their money was. That left Susan with little access to the money that Tom had been building up over the years. Unfortunately, the mounting bills could not wait, and Susan had to go through probate court to claim all the assets that were not in her name. The process dragged on for over a year, during which she had to keep paying property taxes, insurance, and all the other bills.

By the time everything was settled, Susan had spent thousands on legal fees, lost precious time with her family, and felt like her relationship with her kids was never going to be the same. All of this could have been avoided with some simple estate planning.

What is Estate Planning, Really?

Estate planning is a fancy term for a simple idea: It's the plan you make for what happens to your stuff, your loved ones, and your wishes when you're no longer around to make those decisions yourself. It's not just about dividing up your possessions. It's about making sure your family is cared for, your assets go where you want them to, and your values are respected.

Let's break it down. Your estate isn't just your house or your bank account. It includes everything you own: your car, your furniture, your retirement savings, and even your social media accounts. Yes, those Facebook photos and old tweets are part of your digital estate! Estate planning ensures that all of these things are handled the way *you* want.

However, estate planning also goes deeper than that. It's about answering questions like:

- Who will take care of my kids or pets if I'm not here?

- What kind of medical treatment would I want if I couldn't make decisions for myself?

- How can I avoid unnecessary taxes and legal fees for my loved ones?

The Building Blocks of Estate Planning

When you boil it down, estate planning consists of a few key elements:

1. **A Will**:

    - This is your basic roadmap for what happens to your belongings and who will take care of any dependents. It's step one in making sure your wishes are respected.

2. **A Trust**:

    - Trusts might sound like something only billionaires use. Still, they're for anyone who wants to avoid probate court, protect their privacy, or set conditions for distributing their assets.

3. **Powers of Attorney**:

    - There are two main kinds: financial and healthcare. These documents let someone you trust make decisions for you if you can't.

4. **Beneficiary Designations**:

   - Many assets, like life insurance policies and retirement accounts, must pass through a will. They go directly to the people you've named as beneficiaries. Keeping these up to date is critical. A version of beneficiaries called a Transfer on Death (TOD) Registration can be added to Non-Retirement accounts.

5. **Advance Directives**:

   - These documents, like a living will or healthcare proxy, outline your medical wishes if you are unable to communicate them.

Each tool serves a specific purpose but creates a safety net for you and your loved ones.

Why It's Important to Start Now

If Tom and Susan's story taught us anything, it's that not planning is still a plan—it's just bad. Without a will or trust, your estate is handled according to the laws in your state, not your personal wishes. That can lead to outcomes you never wanted, like assets going to distant relatives instead of close friends or your family battling over decisions in court.

But here's the good news: estate planning is simpler than it sounds. The hardest part is starting. Once you take that first step, the rest is just about adding pieces to your plan over time.

Common Misconceptions About Estate Planning

Let's tackle some of the myths that hold people back from getting started:

- **"I'm too young for this."** You might think estate planning is something to worry about later in life. Still, accidents and illnesses (like Tom's) can happen at any age. Estate planning isn't about expecting the worst; it's about being prepared if the worst happens.

- **"I don't own enough to need a plan."** Estate planning isn't just for the wealthy. If you have a car, a bank account, or even a favorite collection of baseball cards, you have an estate.

- **"It's too expensive."** Yes, estate planning can cost money, but it doesn't have to break the bank. And the cost of not planning? That can be much higher—both financially and emotionally.

- **"I don't want to think about dying."** Estate planning isn't about death. It's about protecting the people and things that matter most to you.

How Estate Planning Protects Your Loved Ones

One of the most significant benefits of estate planning is how it helps the people you leave behind. When you don't have a plan, your family has to pick up the pieces. That means navigating court systems, paying legal fees, and often dealing with family drama—all while grieving your loss.

Imagine if Tom and Susan had sat down one weekend to create a simple will and update their beneficiary designations. It would have taken just a few hours, but it could have saved Susan months of stress and thousands of dollars. Their kids could have focused on celebrating Tom's life instead of fighting over his belongings. That's the power of estate planning.

Action Steps to Get Started

By now, you might be wondering, "What do I need to do first?" Don't worry—this isn't about overhauling your life in one sitting. Start small with these three steps:

1. **Make a List of Your Assets**:
    - Include everything you own, from your house and car to your bank accounts and retirement funds. Don't forget digital assets like email accounts and online subscriptions.

2. **Think About Your Priorities**:

    ◦ Who do you want to inherit your belongings? Who would you trust to make medical or financial decisions for you? Write down your answers.

3. **Schedule a Planning Session**:

    ◦ Whether with a professional or just a quiet hour at your kitchen table, set aside time to start putting your wishes into writing.

A Better Future for You and Your Family

Estate planning isn't about how much you have—it's about how much you care. It's the ultimate way to show love and responsibility to the people who matter most to you. So, let's not wait until it's too late. Take that first step today and give yourself and your family the gift of peace of mind.

And hey, if you're feeling overwhelmed, remember: you're not alone. This book is here to guide you every step of the way. By the end of this journey, you'll not only understand estate planning—you'll have a solid foundation that you can build on for years to come.

So, let's keep going and take the next step together. Your loved ones will thank you.

Chapter Three

The Essential Documents You Need

Let's take a moment to imagine something. Picture your family sitting around your dining table. Maybe they're laughing about your favorite jokes or arguing about who should've won that last board game. Now, imagine the mood shifts because there's no plan for what happens to everything you've worked so hard for. That's what estate planning protects against. It makes sure that instead of chaos and confusion, your family has clarity and peace.

And it all starts with five key documents. Don't worry—these aren't as intimidating as they might sound. Think of them as tools that let you take control. Together, they'll help you protect your assets, honor your wishes, and make life easier for those you love.

The Heart of Your Estate Plan: Five Key Documents

Let's start with the big picture: what happens if you don't have these documents? Without a will or a plan, the court decides who gets your stuff and manages everything. They don't know—or care—who you promised your watch or wedding ring to. Worse, if you're incapacitated, no one will know what kind of medical care you want, leaving your family to make impossible decisions.

The good news? These five documents make sure none of that happens. They put the power in your hands.

The Last Will and Testament

Think of your will as your "final say." The document spells out who gets what and who's in charge of making it happen. Want your sister to have your house? Done. Want your best friend to take care of your dog? No problem. Your will ensures your wishes are followed. This is important because if you don't have a will, the court steps in, and their decisions might not align with yours. For example, if you're married with kids from a previous relationship, the court might split your estate in ways you didn't intend.

Now, I want you to think about Florence Griffith-Joyner—FloJo, the Olympic gold medalist. FloJo reportedly had a will, but it couldn't be found after her sudden death. Without that document, her family had to endure years of court battles to settle her estate. A simple step like ensuring her will was accessible could've saved her family so much pain.

And here's a bonus: If you have minor kids, your will is where you name their guardians. Imagine the peace of mind knowing your kids will be cared for by someone you trust.

Power of Attorney (POA)

A Power of Attorney lets someone you trust step in to manage your finances if you can't. Maybe you're in a coma or recovering from surgery and can't keep up with bills. Your POA ensures your electricity doesn't get shut off and your taxes are paid on time.

But here's the thing, not just anyone can handle this role. You need someone responsible who understands how you manage your money and can make decisions in your best interest. This isn't about picking favorites—it's about choosing the best person to handle the job.

Medical Power of Attorney

Think of the Medical Power of Attorney as the companion to your healthcare directive (covered in the next section). While your Power Of Attorney allows someone to act on your behalf for Financial and Legal matters, the Medical POA gives someone the authority to act on your behalf for Medical and Health matters if you're unable to communicate. This person will be your advocate, ensuring doctors follow your wishes.

Here's where it gets tricky: choosing the right person. Your Medical POA needs to be someone who can handle tough conversations with doctors and make decisions that align with your values, even if it's hard.

Pro Tip: Have an honest conversation with this person beforehand. Let them know what you want and why so they feel confident stepping into this role.

Healthcare Directive (Living Will)

Now, let's talk about one of the most emotionally charged documents in your estate plan: the healthcare directive. This is where you spell out your medical wishes—things like whether you want to be on life support or if you'd prefer hospice care.

Margaret was the kind of woman everyone in the neighborhood admired. At 78, she was active in her community, loved gardening, and cherished time with her two daughters, Beth and Emily. While she had slowed down a little in recent years, Margaret always seemed to have her affairs in order—or so her daughters thought.

One winter, Margaret had a severe stroke that left her unable to communicate. In the days that followed, the doctors explained that her condition was critical and decisions about her care needed to be made quickly. That's when the cracks in her otherwise well-organized life began to show.

Beth, the older daughter, believed that their mother wouldn't want to be kept alive on machines. "Mom always said she didn't want to linger if her quality of life was gone," she insisted. Emily, the younger daughter, disagreed. "Mom's a fighter," she argued. "We should do everything possible to give her a chance to recover."

The sisters clashed, each convinced they were honoring their mother's wishes. The tension grew unbearable as the hospital pressured them to make a decision. The responsibility fell entirely on them, and no advance directive or healthcare proxy was in place. What should have been a time for supporting each other and comforting their mother became a source of deep conflict.

After weeks of arguments and second-guessing, the family reluctantly agreed to withdraw life support. But the emotional toll lingered. Beth and Emily couldn't shake the feeling that they might have made the wrong choice. Their relationship, once close, was strained by resentment and guilt.

The Takeaway

Margaret's story is a heartbreaking example of what can happen when healthcare wishes aren't documented clearly. If Margaret had created an Advanced Healthcare Directive and Healthcare Power of Attorney, her daughters wouldn't have been left to guess. They could have focused on being there for their mom instead of being consumed by doubt and conflict.

This story reminds us that planning for healthcare decisions is just as important as financial planning. Outlining your wishes now can spare your loved ones unnecessary pain and ensure your choices are respected.

Revocable Living Trust

Finally, we have the trust. A trust isn't just for the wealthy—it's for anyone who wants to avoid probate, keep their estate private, and make things easier for their family. Think of a trust as a container for your assets. You decide what goes in it, how it's managed, and who gets what when you're gone.

Here's a real-world example: If you own a house, putting it in a trust means your family can bypass probate and take ownership quickly. They might be stuck in court for months—or even years without a trust.

The Danger of Procrastination

Let's take a moment to address something most people don't want to admit: procrastination. It's easy to think, "I'll get to this later." But the truth is, life sometimes doesn't give us a heads-up.

I had a friend named John who always said he'd handle his estate plan "next year." He was healthy, in his 40s, and thought he had plenty of time. Then, a car accident changed everything. After the accident, John's first wife, who he hadn't seen in years, tried to claim that she was a beneficiary of his estate. Gena, John's second wife and mother to his two children, had to navigate months of legal red tape to access the entire estate because John didn't have a will or trust. It was a nightmare she didn't need while grieving.

The lesson? Don't wait. Estate planning is about protecting your loved ones, and there's no better time to start than right now.

Your Next Step

Here's what I want you to do: Grab a piece of paper or open your notes app. Write down the names of five people:

1. Someone to handle your finances (POA).

2. Someone to advocate for your medical care (Medical POA).

3. A guardian for your kids or pets.

4. An executor to carry out your will.

5. A backup for any of the above.

This isn't a final decision—it's just a starting point. Once you've got these names down, you're already ahead of the game.

Estate planning doesn't have to be overwhelming. With these five documents, you're building a solid foundation that protects your family, your assets, and your peace of mind. And trust me, they'll thank you for it.

Chapter Four

Debunking Common Misconceptions About Estate Planning

Let's face it: when you hear "estate planning," it's easy to picture a billionaire in a high-rise office dividing up yachts and Swiss bank accounts. For most people, estate planning feels like something reserved for the ultra-wealthy, the elderly, or the overly prepared. And that's precisely why so many people put it off.

However, those ideas about estate planning? They're myths. Misconceptions. And they can cost you—and your family—a lot more than you might think. So, let's bust some of these myths right here and now. By the end of this chapter, you'll see that estate planning isn't just for 'those people.' It's for you. And once you understand this, you'll feel a sense of relief, knowing that you're not alone in this and that there's a way to protect what you have.

Myth #1: "I Don't Have Enough to Need an Estate Plan"

This is the most common misconception. People think, "I don't own a mansion or have millions in the bank—why bother?" But estate planning isn't about how much you have; it's about protecting what you do have.

Imagine this. You've got a small savings account, a car, and maybe a couple of sentimental items like Grandma's china or your prized fishing rod. Now, imagine you don't have a plan in place. Who gets those things? Without a will, the court decides. And trust me, the court doesn't know—or care—that you wanted your niece to have the china because she's the only one who knows the family recipes.

Here's a real kicker. Even if you think you have "nothing," you probably have more than you realize. Do you have a bank account? A retirement plan? Life insurance? All of that is part of your estate and worth planning for.

Myth #2: "Estate Planning is Only for Older People"

Let me be blunt: if you're over 18, you need at least a basic estate plan. Why? Because accidents and illnesses don't care about your age.

Take Florence Griffin Joyner, the 3 time Olympic Gold medalist and multiple world record holder. In September 1998, at the age of 38, she died in her sleep from an Epileptic seizure. She was at the peak of health and just 5 years away from her Gold medal performances in the 1993 Olympics. Now Flo-Jo, as she was called, had a will. However, no one could find it after she died, sparking years of court battles to settle her estate. Life happens, and it can happen to anyone regardless of age or physical health. That is why you need to prepare.

The takeaway here is simple. You're never too young to make your wishes clear. A proper Estate Plan can save your family from heartbreak and endless legal costs. By taking action now, you're not only protecting your assets but also empowering yourself with the confidence that your wishes will be respected.

Myth #3: "A Will is All I Need"

Don't get me wrong—a Will is a great starting point. But it's not the whole picture. A will doesn't cover things like who can make medical decisions for you if you're incapacitated or how your assets are managed if you're still alive but unable to handle them yourself.

Think of your estate plan as a team. Your Will is the star player, but it needs backup—things like a power of attorney, a Medical Power of Attorney, a healthcare directive, and a trust—to cover all the bases.

Here's another thing to keep in mind: certain assets, like retirement accounts and life insurance, don't follow your Will. They follow beneficiary designations. So, if you named your ex-spouse as your 401(k) beneficiary ten years ago and never updated it, guess who's getting that money? (Hint: It's not your current spouse.) A comprehensive estate plan ensures nothing slips through the cracks. When we work with clients at my firm, we review beneficiaries every year with our clients, even if it annoys them. A little later in the book, I will share a story of why I am so obsessive about beneficiaries (it will chill you to the bone). But with a comprehensive estate plan, you can rest easy, knowing that everything is in order and your loved ones will be taken care of.

Myth #4: "Estate Planning is Too Expensive"

Okay, let's talk money. Yes, hiring an estate attorney can cost a few hundred—or even a few thousand—dollars. But here's the thing: the cost of not planning can be far higher.

Probate fees, legal battles, and taxes can consume a significant chunk of your estate—and that's not even counting the emotional cost to your family. Think about it. Would you rather spend a little now to create a plan or risk leaving your loved ones with a financial and emotional mess?

The good news? Estate planning doesn't have to break the bank. There are affordable options, like DIY tools for basic plans or legal aid programs for more complex needs. The key is to do something. Even a simple plan is better than no plan at all.

Myth #5: "I'll Just Let My Family Figure It Out"

Let me be crystal clear. This is the worst myth of them all. Leaving your family to "figure it out" is a recipe for disaster. Without clear instructions, even the closest families can find themselves at odds.

Here's a story to illustrate the point. A friend of mine—we'll call her Lisa—lost her father unexpectedly. He didn't have a will or any estate planning documents. Lisa and her siblings spent months arguing over how to divide their belongings, even to the point of two siblings fighting over dad's worn-out couch. They didn't seem to appreciate my suggestion to chainsaw it down the middle. What should've been a time for grieving and remembering their dad turned into a battleground. And here's the thing. Their dad wasn't wealthy. It wasn't about money—it was about emotions. Who got the family photo albums? Who got the antique clock? These fights tore the family apart.

Estate planning isn't just about money. It's about leaving a clear roadmap, so your family doesn't have to navigate the emotional minefield of making decisions without your input.

Why These Myths Persist

So, why do these myths stick around? Part of it is fear. Let's be honest—thinking about death or incapacity isn't exactly fun. But avoiding the topic doesn't make it go away. In fact, it usually makes things worse.

Another reason is misinformation. A lot of people don't know what estate planning is or how it works. They think it's too complicated, expensive, or unnecessary. That's why this chapter exists—to show you that estate planning is none of those things. It's simple, doable, and one of the most loving things you can do for your family.

The Truth About Estate Planning

Here's the bottom line. Estate planning isn't about age, wealth, or status. It's about making choices now to protect your loved ones later. It's about ensuring your voice is heard, your wishes are respected, and your family is cared for.

So, if you've been putting it off because of one of these myths, let this be your wake-up call. You don't need to be a billionaire, a senior citizen, or a legal expert to create an estate plan. You just need to care enough about your family to start.

Your Next Step

Here's a quick exercise to get you started. Grab a pen and paper—or open your notes app—and answer these three questions:

1. Who would I trust to handle my finances if something happened to me tomorrow?

2. Who would I want to make medical decisions on my behalf?

3. What's one thing I own that I want to make sure goes to a specific person?

That's it. Just three questions. Once you've answered them, you've taken the first step toward busting these myths and creating a plan that works for you.

Estate planning doesn't have to be complicated. It just takes a little time, a little effort, and a lot of love for the people who matter most. Let's keep going—there's so much more to learn, and we're just starting.

Chapter Five

How to Avoid Probate

Let me introduce you to Karen. Karen was a devoted daughter, always there for her dad through thick and thin. When her father passed away suddenly, Karen assumed that everything he owned—his modest house, his savings, even the old family car—would naturally transfer to her and her siblings. After all, they were his kids, and he hadn't remarried after Karen's mom passed years earlier. But Karen didn't know that her father's estate had to go through probate because he didn't have a trust or other tools to bypass it. This could have been avoided if they had taken early action to plan his estate.

What followed was a nightmare. Karen spent over a year tied up in court hearings, filling out endless paperwork, and paying thousands of dollars in attorney fees—all while grieving her father. And because probate is a public process, every detail of her family's finances became part of the public record. Strangers and distant relatives who hadn't been around in decades suddenly felt entitled to voice their opinions about how the estate should be divided.

Karen told me later, "I just wanted to focus on saying goodbye to my dad. Instead, it felt like I was fighting the system every step of the way." That experience left her exhausted and disillusioned.

Now, contrast Karen's story with Mike's. Mike's mom, Carol, had a very different approach. Carol wasn't wealthy but had worked with an estate planner to set up a living trust. When Carol passed, Mike and his siblings were able to handle her estate quickly and quietly. No court, no public records, no delays. The relief? Carol had a plan.

So, what exactly is probate, and why does it create so much chaos? More importantly, how can you avoid it? Let's break it down.

What is Probate, and Why Does It Matter?

Probate is a court process where a judge oversees the distribution of your assets after you pass away. The idea is to ensure that your debts are paid and your remaining property goes to the rightful heirs. On paper, it sounds reasonable. In practice, it can be a mess.

Here's why:

1. **It's Slow**: The probate process can drag on for months or even years. During that time, your family may be unable to access funds or sell property they might desperately need.

2. **It's Expensive**: Probate fees—court costs, lawyer fees, appraiser fees—can add up quickly, often eating away at your estate's value.

3. **It's Public**: Probate records are open to the public, meaning anyone can see the details of your estate. For some families, this invites unwanted attention or even disputes.

Let me share another story to illustrate this point. Remember Prince? The legendary musician who left behind an estate worth over $150 million? Despite his fame and fortune, Prince didn't leave a will. When he passed away unexpectedly, his estate entered probate, sparking years of legal battles among his potential heirs. Lawyers and administrators drained millions from the estate in fees. As of this writing, the case still needs to be fully resolved. Think about that: a fortune tied up for years because there wasn't a plan.

However, probate issues are not just for the rich. Let me give you a personal example. My mother-in-law died earlier this year. She did not have much; we had all her documents in place (i.e., Will, Powers of Attorney, and Medical Directives). She lived in New Mexico, which has one of the most straightforward processes for probate of small estates like hers. It can be done all DIY, and it costs just $40 to file the case with the state. I knew I was willing to do the work and save my brother-in-law some money. The process was simple and straightforward, giving me the confidence to handle it.

Be careful when you assume. As I got into the process, I realized that the property was in my father-in-law's name (who had died in 2010), and the house was in my mother-in-law's name. After my father-in-law's death, his estate was never probated, and after two years, you can not use the simple $40 process. What I thought would be easy and inexpensive has become almost a year of working through the process and thousands of dollars to fix what should have been a simple process. Unfortunately, I was not involved in helping my in-laws put together their estate plans (they actually had most of the appropriate documents). A simple revocable trust that they could have drawn up for less than $400 in some cases would have eliminated all the issues that we are facing.

Probate isn't inherently bad—it's designed to protect creditors and ensure fairness—but it's almost always avoidable. And for most people, avoiding it is the better option.

The Tools to Avoid Probate

The good news is, you don't have to leave your loved ones stuck in probate court. There are several tools you can use to bypass the process entirely. Let's walk through them with a few stories to show how they work in real life.

Revocable Living Trusts: The Probate Bypass

Imagine you've spent your whole life building a legacy—a house, some savings, maybe a small business. You want those assets to pass smoothly to your loved ones. A revocable living trust is like creating a private roadmap for your assets. You transfer ownership of your assets to the trust, and when you pass, the trust dictates how those assets are distributed.

Here's how it worked for Carol, Mike's mom. Carol owned a small rental property in addition to her primary home. When she created her trust, she transferred both properties into it. By doing this, she ensured that her kids wouldn't have to wait for a court's approval to take ownership. Instead, as the trustee, Mike followed the trust instructions, distributing the properties and other assets according to Carol's wishes. The process was seamless and private, just as Carol intended.

Here's a common mistake. Creating a trust but failing to fund it. Think of it like buying a suitcase but never packing it for the trip. If your assets aren't transferred into the trust, they're still subject to probate. So, once you set up a trust, move your accounts, property titles, and other assets into it.

Beneficiary Designations: A Simple but Powerful Tool

Have you ever filled out a form for a retirement account or life insurance policy and been asked to name a beneficiary? That's because these accounts can bypass probate if you've designated someone to receive them. That is the good part. It is easy, does not cost anything, and beneficiaries can be changed anytime. The bad part? You have to remember to change them if anything in your life changes.

Let me tell you the story of Frank and Anna; they had been married for over 20 years and were each other's soul mates. They had traveled the world together, had three amazing kids, and were planning on having the retirement of their dreams starting in the next couple of years. That was when Frank noticed a stomach pain that wouldn't go away. He was diagnosed with stomach cancer and unfortunately passed away in 6 months. I never met Frank. I came into the picture when Anna, Frank's wife and executrix, called me and wanted to discuss reregistering his large 401k in her name since she was his wife and beneficiary. That was when the problems began. When the 401k representative with our company pulled up the 401k account, Anna's name was not listed as a beneficiary, only Colleen, his first wife, who he had divorced 30 years prior. Colleen and Frank had one son and had what can best be described as a cantankerous relationship. Frank and his son were estranged and hadn't spoken in over 15 years.

To make a long story short, a lengthy court battle ensued in which Colleen agreed to give up her claim to the entire 401k as long as she and Frank's son immediately received 25% of the account, with the rest going to Anna.

Was this what Frank wanted? We will never know. It was probably the right thing to do, but it could have turned out much worse. Colleen was the sole beneficiary and could have easily left nothing for Anna and her children.

The lesson? Check your beneficiary designations regularly, especially after major life events like marriage, divorce, or the birth of a child. It's a simple step, but it can save your loved ones a lot of heartache.

Payable-on-Death and Transfer-on-Death Accounts

Payable-on-death (POD) or transfer-on-death (TOD) accounts are another easy way to avoid probate. These allow you to name a beneficiary who will inherit the account directly upon your passing. Think of it like handing someone a key to a safety deposit box—once you're gone, they can access it immediately.

Let me tell you about Sarah. Sarah's husband was a client of mine early in my career in finance. Her husband was a deputy sheriff but had inherited a small amount of money in the late 1990s and started trading tech and Dotcom stocks. He was a good trader, taking a modest portfolio from about $100,000 to over $1.6mm at the high point. This large account was in his name only because of the inheritance. One afternoon, I received a call from Sarah that her husband had died in a freak accident at their vacation home. She needed my help getting the accounts in her name. Unfortunately, I had to let her know that since the accounts were in his name only, I couldn't tell her anything about the accounts or reregister them in her name, and she would have to get authorization through the probate court. Her husband had told her where his will was to add to the challenge.

Fast forward 18 months. Sarah was fighting through the probate courts; her husband's account had been assigned to a court-appointed person to oversee it, who had no authorization to make any changes to the accounts. If you know anything about this period, we had seen a significant downturn in the market, specifically in the type of stocks her husband had invested in, and his account was heavily leveraged. Our company was forced to keep selling the investments throughout this period to cover margin requirements. In the end, once Sarah could finally take over the account, it dropped from $1.6mm to just over $100,000, and that was all she had except for a small life insurance policy. In addition, she had an attorney's bill of several thousand dollars to pay. How could this have been solved?

Joint Ownership with Right of Survivorship

If you own property jointly with someone else—like a spouse—the right of survivorship means that ownership automatically transfers to the surviving person when one owner passes. While this is a straightforward way to avoid probate, it's not without risks. Adding someone to a property title could have unintended tax or legal consequences, so it's essential to consult with an expert before making changes.

Give It Away While You're Alive

Sometimes, the simplest way to avoid probate is to give assets to your loved ones while you're still here. My neighbor, Linda, started gifting her prized jewelry collection to her grandchildren during family gatherings. Not only did it bring her joy to see them cherish her treasures, but it also ensured those items wouldn't get tangled up in her estate.

Remember that large gifts may be subject to gift taxes, so check with a financial advisor before transferring significant assets.

The Emotional Toll of Probate

Beyond the legal and financial aspects, probate can take a huge emotional toll on families. Sarah's story is a perfect example. Every court date, delay, and unexpected fee added to her grief. By planning ahead, you're protecting your assets and your family's well-being during one of the most challenging times in their lives.

Your Next Step

Avoiding probate doesn't require a law degree or a fortune—it just requires action. Here's your first step:

1. Make a list of your significant assets.

2. Next to each item, write down who you'd like to inherit it and how it's currently titled.

3. Choose one strategy from this chapter—whether it's creating a trust, updating a beneficiary designation, or setting up a TOD account—and take action this week.

Planning ahead isn't just about saving time and money. It's about giving your family the gift of peace. And trust me, that's worth more than any inheritance.

Chapter Six

Planning for Healthcare and Incapacity

Margaret was the kind of woman everyone in the neighborhood admired. At 78, she was active in her community, loved gardening, and cherished time with her two daughters, Beth and Emily. While she had slowed down a little in recent years, Margaret always seemed to have her affairs in order—or so her daughters thought.

One winter, Margaret had a severe stroke that left her unable to communicate. In the days that followed, the doctors explained that her condition was critical and decisions about her care needed to be made quickly. That's when the cracks in her otherwise well-organized life began to show.

Beth, the older daughter, believed their mother wouldn't want to be kept alive on machines. "Mom always said she didn't want to linger if her quality of life was gone," she insisted. Emily, the younger daughter, disagreed. "Mom's a fighter," she argued. "We should do everything possible to give her a chance to recover."

The sisters clashed, each convinced they were honoring their mother's wishes. The tension grew unbearable as the hospital pressured them to make a decision. The responsibility fell entirely on them, and no advance directive or healthcare proxy was in place. What should have been a time for supporting each other and comforting their mother became a source of deep conflict.

After weeks of arguments and second-guessing, the family reluctantly agreed to withdraw life support. But the emotional toll lingered. Beth and Emily couldn't shake the feeling that they might have made the wrong choice. Their relationship, once close, was strained by resentment and guilt.

The Takeaway

Margaret's story is a heartbreaking example of what can happen when healthcare wishes aren't documented clearly. If Margaret had created an Advanced Healthcare Directive and Healthcare Power of Attorney, her daughters wouldn't have been left to guess. They could have focused on being there for their mom instead of being consumed by doubt and conflict. The relief that comes with clear healthcare planning is immeasurable, sparing your loved ones unnecessary pain and ensuring your choices are respected.

This story reminds us that planning for healthcare decisions is just as important as financial planning. Outlining your wishes now can spare your loved ones unnecessary pain and ensure your choices are respected.

Why Healthcare Planning is Crucial

It's not easy to think about a time when you might be unable to make your own decisions. But life doesn't always give us a choice. Accidents happen. Illnesses strike. And suppose you don't make your wishes known ahead of time. In that case, someone else will have to make those decisions for you—often under enormous emotional stress. However, by making your healthcare wishes known, you can regain a sense of control and empower your loved ones to act on your behalf.

Terri Schiavo's case highlights what can go wrong when those decisions aren't clear. But it's not just about avoiding family fights. It's about ensuring that your voice is heard, even when you can't speak for yourself. The importance of avoiding family disputes in healthcare decisions cannot be overstated, underscoring the need for proactive planning.

The Terri Schiavo Case: A Deep Dive

Let's unpack what happened to Terri because her story is more than just a headline—it's a cautionary tale.

In 1990, Terri collapsed in her home after suffering cardiac arrest, likely due to a potassium imbalance caused by an eating disorder. The lack of oxygen to her brain left her in what doctors described as a persistent vegetative state. She could breathe on her own but required a feeding tube for nutrition and hydration.

Terri's husband, Michael, and her parents, Bob and Mary Schindler, worked together to care for her for years. But as time went on, their views diverged. Michael believed that Terri wouldn't want to live in such a condition. The Schindlers, deeply religious, believed Terri could recover and tried to keep her on life support indefinitely.

In 1998, Michael petitioned the court to have Terri's feeding tube removed, arguing that she had once expressed a desire not to be kept alive artificially. The Schindlers fought back, insisting that Michael was misrepresenting her wishes and had a conflict of interest. What followed was a legal battle that spanned nearly seven years, involved multiple court rulings, and became a lightning rod for political and cultural debates.

- **The Medical Debate**: Doctors couldn't agree on Terri's prognosis. Some believed her condition was irreversible, while others claimed she might improve with therapy.

- **The Legal Battle**: Florida courts sided with Michael, but the Schindlers appealed repeatedly, delaying the removal of the feeding tube.

- **The Public Outcry**: The case became a media sensation, with activists, religious groups, and politicians taking sides. Protesters gathered outside Terri's hospice, and her case was debated on talk shows and news outlets nationwide.

- **Congress Gets Involved**: In an unprecedented move, Congress passed a bill allowing federal courts to review the case.

President George W. Bush signed it into law, but federal courts ultimately upheld the decision to remove the feeding tube.

In March 2005, after years of legal battles and public scrutiny, Terri's feeding tube was removed for the final time. She passed away 13 days later. Her case remains a powerful example of how deeply personal decisions can spiral out of control without clear directives.

What Can We Learn from Terri's Story?

Terri's case teaches us two critical lessons:

1. **Make Your Wishes Known**: Terri didn't have a healthcare directive, so her family was left guessing what she would have wanted. A healthcare directive is a written document that outlines your preferences for medical treatment if you cannot communicate.

2. **Appoint a Medical Power of Attorney**: By naming someone you trust to make medical decisions on your behalf, you can avoid family disputes and ensure that your wishes are respected.

The Tools You Need

When it comes to planning for healthcare and incapacity, you need two key documents: a healthcare directive and a medical power of attorney. Let's break them down.

Healthcare Directive

A healthcare directive, also known as a living will, is your chance to spell out exactly what kind of medical treatment you want—or don't want—in specific situations. It answers questions like:

- Do you want to be kept alive on life support if there's no chance of recovery?

- Would you prefer hospice care over aggressive treatments at the end of life?

- Are there specific treatments, like blood transfusions or feeding tubes, that you want to avoid?

A healthcare directive takes the guesswork out of tough decisions. It's not just about sparing your family from making those calls—it's about making sure your wishes are honored.

Medical Power of Attorney

A medical power of attorney is the person you choose to make healthcare decisions for you if you cannot do so. This person, often called your healthcare proxy, steps in when your healthcare directive doesn't cover a specific situation or when immediate decisions need to be made.

Choosing the right person for this role is crucial. They should be someone you trust completely, someone who understands your values and will advocate for your wishes—even if it's hard.

The person who is your Medical Power of Attorney does not necessarily have to be who you appoint for your Durable Power of Attorney dealing with your Financial and Legal matters. Let's assume you have two children, one of whom is better with finances while the other is more detail-oriented and would be better at handling healthcare decisions. Splitting up the duties into what they will be best at will help reduce conflicts and the feeling that one person is doing everything.

How to Choose Your Healthcare Proxy

Let me share a story about Sam and Jenny. Sam was a widower in his 60s who appointed his daughter, Jenny, as his healthcare proxy. Jenny adored her father but had a hard time confronting the realities of his end-of-life wishes. When Sam developed a terminal illness, his healthcare directive specified that he didn't want aggressive treatments. But when the time came to make decisions, Jenny struggled to follow his wishes. She felt guilty and wanted to pursue every possible treatment, even if it went against Sam's instructions.

It wasn't until Sam's best friend gently reminded Jenny of her father's wishes that she found the courage to honor them. While Sam had chosen someone he trusted, he hadn't fully prepared her for the emotional weight of the role.

Key Takeaway: When choosing a healthcare proxy, pick someone who is reliable and emotionally strong. Have an open conversation with them about your wishes and the importance of following them, even when it's difficult.

The Emotional Toll of Unclear Decisions

Healthcare decisions are inherently emotional. Without clear instructions, your loved ones can interpret what they think you would want, which can lead to conflict, guilt, and even resentment.

Think about Terri Schiavo's parents and husband. They both believed they were doing what was best for her, but their opposing views created a rift that never healed. By making your wishes clear in advance, you can spare your family from this kind of turmoil.

How to Get Started

Planning for healthcare and incapacity doesn't have to be overwhelming. Here's a step-by-step guide to help you get started:

1. **Reflect on Your Values**: What matters most to you? Do you prioritize quality of life over longevity? Are there specific treatments you feel strongly about?

2. **Write It Down**: Use a healthcare directive form to outline your preferences. Many states provide free templates online.

3. **Choose Your Proxy**: Select someone you trust to make decisions on your behalf. Make sure they're willing and able to take on the role.

4. **Have the Conversation**: Talk to your proxy, your family, and your healthcare providers about your wishes. The more people who understand your plan, the better.

5. **Update Regularly**: Life circumstances change. Review your documents every few years or after significant life events.

The Peace of Mind You Deserve

By taking these steps, you're not just planning for the worst—you're giving yourself and your loved ones peace of mind. You're ensuring your voice will be heard no matter what happens. And you're sparing your family from the kind of pain and conflict that defined Terri Schiavo's story.

Remember, planning for healthcare and incapacity isn't just a practical decision—it's loving. It's a way to care for your family, even when you can't speak for yourself.

Chapter Seven

Family Dynamics and Communication

Picture this. You're at a family dinner again. The table is filled with the usual chatter—your son-in-law talking about his latest project, your grandkids arguing over who gets the last slice of pie. Everything feels routine, even comforting. Imagine dropping this question into the middle: "So, let's talk about what happens when I'm gone."

Awkward, right? The proverbial flatulence in church. No one wants to think about these conversations, let alone have them. But here's the truth: if you don't talk about it now, your family might deal with far worse down the road.

Let me tell you about a family I knew—the Bennetts. Margaret and Paul were the kind of parents everyone admired. They were loving, practical, and always looking out for their three kids. But when it came to estate planning, they made the same mistake many people do. They avoided talking about it. Margaret thought it would be uncomfortable, and Paul figured the kids would just figure things out when the time came.

They didn't. When Margaret and Paul passed within a few years of each other, their kids found themselves at odds over almost everything—who would handle the estate, whether to sell the family home and even who got the heirloom grandfather clock. Old rivalries bubbled to the surface. By the time the estate was settled, relationships had frayed, and family gatherings became rare and awkward.

That's the kind of story we all want to avoid, right? The good news is you can prevent it. But it starts with a conversation. This open dialogue can bring a sense of relief, knowing that everyone's concerns and wishes are being heard and considered.

Why Families Struggle to Talk About Estate Plans

Let's be honest—talking about estate planning isn't anyone's idea of a good time. It's like discussing taxes or cholesterol over a glass of wine. Most people avoid it because it feels uncomfortable or they think it will stir up drama.

But here's the thing. Avoiding the conversation doesn't make the issues go away. It leaves your family to deal with them later, often when emotions are already high. It was easy and far less uncomfortable for you, but not so good for them. That's a recipe for misunderstandings, resentment, and even outright conflict.

Take Emily and Brian, for example. Their father passed away without ever explaining why he'd named Emily as the executor of his will. Brian, the younger sibling, assumed it was favoritism—proof that their dad had always trusted Emily more. Their father chose Emily because she lived nearby and had experience managing paperwork. However, Brian spent months stewing over perceived slights because he never explained his reasoning. Their relationship hasn't been the same since.

See how easily things can spiral? That's why having a conversation isn't just helpful—it's essential. Having done this job for over 30 years now, I have seen it time and again with clients' family members. All those little things that annoyed you about your siblings in the past can come to a head when mom and dad are no longer around to be the buffer.

Making the Conversation Easier

I know what you think: "I don't want to cause drama." Or maybe, "What if they don't like my decisions?" Let me tell you something: your family might not agree with everything in your estate plan, and that's okay. The goal isn't to make everyone happy but to ensure everyone understands.

One way to ease into the conversation is by sharing your intentions. For example, if you've named one child as the executor, explain why. Say something like, "I chose you because you're good with details, and I trust you to handle this responsibly. It's not about favoritism—it's about what makes the most sense." When you're open about your reasoning, it helps your family see your choices as practical rather than personal, and it empowers them to understand and respect your decisions.

Another tip? Choose the right time and setting. This isn't a conversation to have during Thanksgiving dinner or in the middle of a family crisis. Pick a quiet, neutral moment when everyone can focus. I've known families tackling this over coffee on a Sunday morning or during a casual walk. The key is to create an atmosphere where everyone feels comfortable.

What Happens When You Don't Talk

Let's revisit the Bennetts for a moment. Their son, David, always assumed he'd inherit the family home. He'd helped his parents renovate it and even had plans to move in one day. However, Margaret and Paul had left the house to their daughter, Lisa, who had been struggling financially and needed stability.

When David found out, he was furious—not because he didn't care about Lisa, but because he felt blindsided. "If they had just told me," he said, "I would've understood. But finding out like this made me feel they didn't trust me."

This is what happens when families don't talk. Minor misunderstandings become big issues. Resentment builds. And the focus shifts from honoring a loved one's wishes to dealing with hurt feelings.

How Communication Brings Families Together

Now, let me tell you about the Carters. When Jim and Linda finalized their estate plan, they decided to involve their two kids, Rachel and Ben, in the process. They sat them down one evening and said, "We want to talk about what happens when we're gone—not because we're planning on going anywhere anytime soon, but because we want everything to be clear."

Jim explained that Rachel would be the executor because she was meticulous and good with details. Ben, who had a knack for investing, would help manage the trust. Then, they talked about the house, the savings, and even the family's prized collection of antique books. They explained their reasoning for every decision and invited Rachel and Ben to share their thoughts. This involvement not only ensured everyone's understanding but also strengthened the family bond.

Were there some disagreements? Sure. But by the end of the conversation, everyone understood the plan. More importantly, everyone felt included. When Jim and Linda eventually passed, Rachel and Ben worked together seamlessly. The estate was settled without drama, and the family bond remained intact.

This is the power of communication. It doesn't eliminate every potential conflict but sets the stage for understanding, respect, and collaboration.

Addressing Sensitive Topics

Of course, not every conversation will go as smoothly as the Carters'. Some families have deep-seated tensions or complicated dynamics. Maybe one sibling has always felt left out or has a history of financial disputes. These situations require extra care.

If you're dealing with a sensitive topic, approach it with empathy and acknowledge the emotions involved. For example, you might say, "I know this isn't easy to talk about, but I want to make sure everyone understands my intentions. This isn't about playing favorites—it's about what makes sense for our family as a whole."

In some cases, bringing in a neutral party can help. A financial advisor or estate attorney can act as a mediator, keeping the conversation focused and fair. Sometimes, having a third party explain your plan can make it feel less personal and more objective.

Your Legacy of Clarity

Ultimately, estate planning isn't just about dividing assets—it's about creating a legacy of clarity and care. It's about showing your family that you've thought everything through and that your decisions come from a place of love.

When you communicate your plan, you're giving your family a gift that goes beyond money or property. You're giving them the tools to work together, honor your wishes, and avoid the kind of pain and conflict that tears families apart.

So, how do you start? It doesn't have to be complicated. Start small, start simple, but start.

Here's how to take action today:

- **Get clear on your message**: Write down the key points you want to share with your family. Think about your choices for executors, trustees, and guardians. Reflect on how you've divided your assets and why.

- **Choose the right moment**: Find a quiet, low-pressure time to talk—maybe a casual weekend gathering or a one-on-one conversation. If your family lives far apart, a video call works just as well.

- **Start the conversation**: Keep it simple. Say, "I've been working on my estate plan, and I want to make sure everyone understands what's in it and why I've made certain decisions." Stay open, listen to concerns, and clarify as needed.

Remember, the hardest part is starting. Once you've opened the door to communication, you'll find it gets easier. And the peace of mind that comes from knowing your family understands your wishes? That's priceless.

Make a Difference with Your Review

Unlock the Power of Generosity

"What we do for ourselves dies with us. What we do for others and the world remains and is immortal." – Albert Pine

People who take a moment to give back, even in small ways, make the world a better place. So, let's make a difference together!

Would you help someone just like you—someone curious about estate planning but unsure where to start?

My mission with *Estate Planning Essentials* is to make the process simple, stress-free, and even a little fun for everyone. But to reach more people who need this information, I need your help.

Most people pick books based on reviews. That's why I'm asking you to lend a hand by leaving your thoughts about this book.

It won't cost you anything but a moment of your time, and your review could make all the difference for someone who's feeling overwhelmed about where to begin.

Your review could help:

- ...one more family avoid unnecessary stress.

- ...one more parent ensure their children are protected.

- ...one more person feel confident about their legacy.

- ...one more loved one navigate the hardest times with ease.

Leaving a review is quick and easy. Just scan the QR code or visit the link below to share your thoughts:

https://www.amazon.com/review/review-your-purchases/?asin=B0DPVVLGHH

If you love helping others, you're my kind of person. Thank you for supporting this mission and for helping others take control of their future.

From the bottom of my heart, thank you!

Jeff Kikel

p.s. If you haven't had a chance to visit our resource page for the book and download your FREE resources, please go to:

https://www.surehorizonretirement.com/estate-planning-essentials

Chapter Eight

Creating a Will That Reflects Your Wishes

Let me introduce you to two very different families. The first is the Millers. Robert and Elaine Miller were devoted parents who worked hard their entire lives to provide for their two children, Amanda and James. They built a comfortable life—a modest home, a bit of savings, and some sentimental items that had been in the family for generations. Robert and Elaine always talked about wanting their children to inherit equally, but they never actually put those wishes into a will. "They know what we want," Robert would say, waving off the topic whenever it came up.

When Elaine passed away unexpectedly, Robert's health began to decline quickly. Within a year, he too was gone, leaving Amanda and James to sort out their parents' estate. What followed was a nightmare. Without a will, the state stepped in to divide the assets. Every decision required legal intervention, and every step created tension between Amanda and James. Arguments over who should manage the process led to long silences. Even small items—like their mother's wedding ring—became points of contention. By the time the estate was settled, their relationship was irreparably damaged.

Now let me tell you about the Rodriguezes. Carmen and Javier Rodriguez also worked hard to build a comfortable life for their family. But instead of leaving things to chance, they created a will together. They thought carefully about who would inherit what and made decisions with their children's personalities and needs in mind. Before finalizing the document, they sat their kids down to explain their choices, answer questions, and ensure everyone understood their intentions. This open and honest communication was key to avoiding the stress and conflict that often accompany estate settlement. The Rodriguez siblings remained as close as ever, their parents' legacy intact.

Two families. Two very different outcomes. The difference? A will—or the lack of one.

Why a Will Matters

A will isn't just a legal document; it's a roadmap for your family. Without one, the court decides who gets what based on state laws. These laws are rigid, designed for efficiency rather than compassion, and don't account for your family's unique dynamics or what you hold dear. By creating a will, you take back control and empower yourself to ensure your wishes are respected.

Take Chris and Jessica. They were a blended family, each with children from previous marriages. When Jessica passed away suddenly without a will, Chris assumed everything would naturally transfer to him. However, state law divided Jessica's assets between Chris and her biological children, leaving Chris scrambling to secure their shared home. A lengthy legal battle ensued, straining relationships and draining resources. It's a situation that could have been avoided entirely with a simple will.

A will ensures your voice is heard and your wishes are honored, no matter what. It's a way to care for the people you love, even when you're no longer there to guide them. Knowing that your loved ones will be taken care of according to your wishes can bring a profound sense of relief and peace of mind.

What to Include in Your Will

At its core, a will answer three key questions:

1. Who gets what?

2. Who's in charge?

3. Who will care for your dependents?

Let's unpack each of these with real-life examples.

Who Gets What?

When Susan wrote her will, she didn't just think about her financial assets; she also considered the sentimental value of her belongings. She left her jewelry to her daughter, Anna, who had always admired it. Her collection of vinyl records went to her son, Jake, who shared her love of music. Susan's will reflected her personality, her relationships, and the things that mattered most to her.

Contrast that with Paul, who assumed his children would "just figure it out." Paul's three kids spent months arguing over who would inherit his prized fishing boat. The conflict got so heated that the boat ended up sitting in storage, unused and unappreciated until it was eventually sold. Paul's lack of planning turned a cherished family memory into a source of division.

Who's in Charge?

Being an executor is a big responsibility. When Lily named her sister, Clara, executor of her estate, she knew Clara was organized and reliable. What she didn't anticipate was how much work the role would involve. Clara had to manage paperwork, communicate with beneficiaries, and handle legal deadlines—all while grieving her sister.

Lily could have made the process easier by providing clear instructions in her will and discussing the role with Clara beforehand. An executor doesn't have to do it all alone; they can hire professionals to assist. However, the person you choose should be someone who can stay calm under pressure and handle complex tasks with care.

Who Will Care for Your Dependents?

One of the most critical decisions in a will is naming a guardian for your minor children or pets. When Tom and Rachel passed away in a car accident, their two young children were left without clear guidance. Tom's brother and Rachel's sister wanted custody, leading to a bitter court battle. The children, already grieving, were caught in the middle.

In contrast, Mia and David took the time to discuss guardianship with their family. They named Mia's cousin, a schoolteacher with a stable home life, as guardian for their children. They also wrote a letter explaining their decision, ensuring there was no room for misunderstanding. When the time came, the transition was seamless, and their children were cared for in the way Mia and David had intended.

Common Mistakes to Avoid

Certain mistakes can undermine your intentions even when you've taken the important step of creating a will. One of the most common—and costly—is failing to update your will after major life changes.

Take Heath Ledger, for example. The beloved actor, known for his iconic roles, tragically passed away at just 28 years old. Heath had been proactive enough to create a will, but he hadn't updated it since the birth of his daughter, Matilda. His will left everything to his parents and sisters, completely overlooking Matilda because it had been written before her birth.

Although Heath's family ultimately agreed to provide for Matilda, the situation could have turned into a prolonged legal battle. The oversight highlighted how critical it is to revisit your will regularly and ensure it reflects your current life circumstances. Heath's story is a potent reminder that life changes and your estate plan should, too.

Why Regular Updates Matter

Life doesn't stand still, and neither should your will. Marriages, divorces, births, and deaths all impact your estate plan. By keeping it updated, you can ensure your assets go exactly where you want them to and prevent unnecessary complications for your loved ones.

The Emotional Side of Estate Planning

A will isn't just about money or property. It's about love, care, and ensuring the people you leave behind can focus on healing rather than stress. Think of it as your last message to your family—a way to say, "I thought of you. I wanted to make this as easy as possible."

Your Next Steps

Here's how to take action today:

- **List** your assets and who you'd like to inherit them. Be specific, and include sentimental items that hold special meaning.

- **Choose your executor** thoughtfully. Pick someone who is organized, trustworthy, and willing to take on the responsibility.

- **Think about dependents**: If you have minor children or pets, decide who would provide the best care and discuss it with them.

Taking these steps isn't just about protecting your assets—it's about protecting your family. A will is more than a document; it's a gift of clarity and peace.

Chapter Nine

Exploring Trusts and Their Benefits

Let me start with a question: What comes to mind when you think of trust? If you're like most people, you might picture a billionaire shielding their fortune or a sprawling estate with high gates and a staff of lawyers. It's easy to think trusts are just tools for the ultra-wealthy. But here's the truth: trusts aren't about how much money you have—they're about how much control you want over what happens to what you have.

Let me tell you about Mike and Laura to help you understand the power of trust. Mike was a retired firefighter, and Laura was a school secretary. They weren't rich, but they were proud of the life they had built—a modest home, some savings, and their two kids, Emma and Jack. Like many parents, Mike and Laura wanted to ensure their kids were cared for if something happened to them, but they figured a simple will would do the trick.

Then, their neighbor, Ron, shared his story. Ron had lost his wife years earlier and thought his estate plan was rock solid. But when Ron passed, his children discovered his estate had to go through probate. Ron's will was unclear as to who would inherit what in his estate, and he had no trust, so it took over a year for them to access their inheritance. In the meantime, legal fees and court costs ate away a significant chunk of it. Mike and Laura were stunned. "We can't let that happen to our kids," Laura said.

That's when they learned about trusts—and everything changed.

What is a Trust?

Let's break it down. A trust is like a treasure chest for your assets. You put your treasures—your home, your savings, or even sentimental items—into the chest and write instructions about how those treasures should be handled. A trustee carries out these instructions and oversees the chest, ensuring it's opened and distributed exactly as you want.

There are three main roles in a trust:

- **The Grantor**: That's you, the person creating the trust and placing assets into it.

- **The Trustee:** The person or entity responsible for managing the trust according to your instructions.

- **The Beneficiaries**: These are the people or organizations that will benefit from the trust.

Unlike a will, which only takes effect after you pass away, some trusts—like a revocable living trust—can start working while you're still alive. This flexibility and control make trusts one of the most versatile tools in estate planning, empowering you to shape your financial future according to your wishes.

The Benefits of Trusts

Now, you might wonder, "Do I need trust?" The answer depends on your goals. Let's explore some of the key benefits with real-life examples.

Avoiding Probate

One of the most significant advantages of a trust is that it allows your assets to bypass probate—a court-supervised process that can be time-consuming, expensive, and public.

Let me share the story of Dave and Carol. They had set up a revocable living trust as part of their overall estate plan. When Dave passed, Carol was able to access the assets immediately without dealing with probate. The trust ensured privacy and allowed Carol to focus on her grief instead of legal issues. "It was the best decision we ever made," Carol said later. "It saved me so much heartache."

Protecting Minor Children

A trust is an invaluable tool for parents of young children. It ensures their inheritance is managed responsibly until they are old enough to handle it.

Consider Sarah, a single mom with two young daughters. Sarah had a will that left everything to her girls, but when her estate planner explained how trusts worked, she realized the risks of her original plan. Without a trust, her daughters would inherit everything at 18—an age Sarah felt was far too young for such responsibility.

By creating a trust, Sarah was able to specify that her daughters would receive a portion of their inheritance at 25, another portion at 30, and the remainder at 35. Until then, the trust would pay for their education, living expenses, and medical needs. Sarah's trust gave her peace of mind, knowing her daughters would be cared for and their inheritance would be protected.

Protecting Assets from Creditors and Divorce

Trusts can shield assets from creditors, lawsuits, or even the financial consequences of divorce.

Take Jason, a small business owner who wanted to leave a legacy for his son, Daniel. But Jason worried about Daniel's marriage, which was already showing signs of strain. He didn't want half of the inheritance going to his son's ex-wife if the marriage ended in divorce.

With his attorney's help, Jason set up a discretionary trust. The trust gave Daniel access to funds for specific purposes, like buying a home or starting a business, but protected the bulk of the assets. When Daniel eventually went through a divorce, the trust ensured his inheritance remained intact.

Types of Trusts

Not all trusts are created equal. Let's look at some common types and their unique benefits.

Revocable Living Trust

This is the most flexible type of trust. You can change, add, or dissolve it entirely during your lifetime. It's perfect for avoiding probate and maintaining control of your assets while you're alive.

Irrevocable Trust

Once you set up an irrevocable trust, it's set in stone. While this might sound restrictive, it comes with significant benefits, like protecting assets from creditors and reducing estate taxes.

Special Needs Trust

A special needs trust allows you to provide for a loved one with disabilities without affecting their eligibility for government benefits.

Charitable Trust

If giving back is part of your legacy, a charitable trust lets you support causes you care about while enjoying tax benefits.

Misconceptions About Trusts

Many people think trusts are only for the wealthy. This couldn't be further from the truth. Trusts are about control and protection, not the size of your estate. Whether you have $50,000 or $5 million, a trust can help you achieve your goals.

Another common misconception is that trusts are too complicated. While setting up a trust does require some effort, it's a manageable and straightforward process with the right guidance. And the benefits far outweigh the initial time and cost, leaving you feeling confident and capable in managing your estate.

Your Next Steps

Here's how you can take action today:

1. **Think about your goals.** Do you want to avoid probate, protect a loved one, or support a cause? Clarify your priorities.

2. **List your assets.** Identify what you'd like to place in a trust and who you'd like to benefit from.

3. **Consult an expert.** A qualified estate planner or attorney can help you choose the right type of trust for your needs.

By creating a trust, you're protecting your assets, your family, your legacy, and your peace of mind. Trusts aren't just for the wealthy—they're for anyone who wants to ensure their wishes are carried out with care and precision.

Chapter Ten

Addressing Digital Assets and Modern Challenges

Let's start with a story about Lisa, a tech-savvy entrepreneur who ran a thriving online business, owned cryptocurrency, and meticulously documented her life through digital photos. Lisa was also a devoted dog mom to Max, a rambunctious golden retriever who was the center of her world. Lisa had always been organized—she managed her accounts flawlessly and kept a running list of her passwords in a secure app. However, one thing Lisa hadn't thought much about was what would happen to her digital world—or to Max—if she wasn't around to manage them.

When Lisa was unexpectedly diagnosed with a terminal illness, she realized the gaps in her estate planning. Her business, crypto wallets, online subscriptions, and, most importantly, Max—all of these parts of her life needed a plan. "What happens if I'm not here to handle it all?" she asked her estate planner during a tearful meeting.

Lisa's story highlights the challenges we face in today's digital age. Traditional estate planning doesn't always address the complexities of online accounts, digital files, and modern concerns like pet care.

However, with a bit of forethought and planning, Lisa was able to create a strategy that ensured her digital legacy and Max's future were in good hands, empowering her to take control of her own destiny. Let's explore how you can do the same.

What Are Digital Assets?

In today's world, much of our lives exist online. From financial accounts to cherished family photos stored in the cloud, digital assets have become integral to modern estate planning.

So, what exactly counts as a digital asset? It's more than just your Facebook account or the pictures on your phone. Digital assets include:

- **Financial Accounts**: Online banking, investment portfolios, PayPal, Venmo, and cryptocurrency wallets.

- **Social Media Accounts**: Platforms like Instagram, TikTok, and Twitter that may hold sentimental or even monetary value.

- **Media and Subscriptions**: eBooks, music, and movies purchased on Amazon or iTunes, as well as cloud-stored photos or documents.

- **Online Businesses**: Websites, domain names, and e-commerce stores like Etsy or Shopify.

- **Cloud Storage**: Files and photos are stored on platforms like Google Drive, Dropbox, or iCloud.

Digital assets often hold both monetary and sentimental value. But without proper planning, these assets can become inaccessible, lost, or even exploited.

Digital Asset Inventory: Getting Started

Creating a digital asset inventory is the first step in managing your digital legacy. Imagine trying to access a loved one's online bank account without knowing the username or password—it's nearly impossible. A detailed inventory provides clarity and prevents frustration for your heirs.

Step 1: Make a List

Start by listing every digital account you own, from online banking to email and streaming services. For each account, include:

- Username and password.
- Recovery email or phone number.
- Backup codes for two-factor authentication.

Step 2: Secure the List

Store this information in a secure, encrypted location. Password managers like LastPass or Dashlane are excellent tools for keeping sensitive data safe.

Step 3: Update Regularly

Technology evolves quickly, and so do your accounts. It's your responsibility to schedule regular updates to keep your inventory current, ensuring that your digital legacy is always up-to-date and reflective of your current situation.

The Role of a Digital Executor

Just as you appoint an executor for your will, you can name a digital executor to manage your online presence. A digital executor ensures your accounts are handled according to your wishes—transferring ownership, closing accounts, or preserving sentimental files. This person should be someone you trust, who is tech-savvy, and who understands your wishes and values.

Let's revisit Lisa's story. Lisa's estate planner helped her appoint a digital executor, her tech-savvy niece, Emily. Emily was tasked with shutting down Lisa's social media accounts, transferring her crypto assets to her beneficiaries, and ensuring Lisa's business website remained active until it could be sold. Because Lisa had meticulously documented her accounts and instructions, Emily was able to execute Lisa's wishes smoothly, giving Lisa peace of mind during her final days.

Planning for Pets

Now, let's talk about Max. For Lisa, Max wasn't just a pet—he was family. But pets often get overlooked in estate planning. Without a clear plan, pets can end up in shelters or with caretakers who aren't prepared for the responsibility.

Pet Trusts

Lisa's estate planner suggested creating a pet trust, a legal arrangement that sets aside funds for Max's care. The trust named Lisa's best friend, Sarah, Max's caretaker, and allocated $10,000 to cover his food, vet bills, and other expenses. A trustee was also named to oversee the funds and ensure they were used appropriately.

Will Provisions

If a formal trust isn't necessary, you can include a provision in your will that names a caretaker and provides instructions for your pet's care. Be sure to discuss this with the chosen caretaker to ensure they're willing and able to take on the responsibility.

Modern Challenges

Planning for digital assets and pets is just the beginning. The digital age brings unique challenges that require careful consideration.

Identity Theft

Even after someone passes, their identity can be stolen. Unsecured digital accounts can be exploited, leading to financial loss and emotional distress for loved ones. Properly managing and closing accounts can help prevent this.

Evolving Technology

What happens to digital assets stored on platforms that didn't exist when your estate plan was created? The best way to future-proof your plan is to work with an estate planner who stays up-to-date on digital trends and can provide ongoing guidance.

Family Disputes

The sentimental value of digital assets—like family photos or videos—can lead to disputes—clear instructions about who inherits what can prevent unnecessary conflict.

Storytelling: How Lisa's Plan Played Out

When Lisa passed away from a brief battle with cancer, her plan was put to the test. Her digital executor, Emily, logged into Lisa's password manager to access her accounts. She shut down Lisa's social media profiles, transferred her cryptocurrency to the beneficiaries, and ensured Lisa's online business was sold to a trusted colleague.

Meanwhile, Sarah took Max home, where he quickly adjusted to his new life. The funds from Lisa's pet trust covered Max's expenses, ensuring he received the same level of care Lisa had always given him.

Lisa's foresight turned what could have been a stressful situation into a seamless transition. Her family was deeply grateful for the care she took in planning every detail, and they found comfort in knowing that everything was taken care of.

Your Next Steps

If Lisa's story has inspired you, here's how you can take action today:

1. Begin compiling a digital asset inventory. List all your accounts, passwords, and access methods in a secure location.

2. Appoint a digital executor—someone who understands the digital landscape and can carry out your wishes.

3. If you have pets, include them in your estate plan. Decide who will care for them and provide the resources they'll

need.

Digital estate planning might initially feel overwhelming, but it's vital to protecting your legacy in the modern world. By addressing these challenges head-on, you're not just planning for your assets—you're planning for the people and pets who mean the most to you.

Chapter Eleven

Minimizing Taxes Through Strategic Estate Planning

Let me ask you something: How would you feel if part of the legacy you spent your life building went straight to Uncle Sam instead of your family? For a lot of people, estate taxes feel like a bad joke—they've already paid taxes on their earnings, and now the government wants another cut just because they passed away. But here's the thing: it doesn't have to be that way. With some planning, you can minimize these taxes and ensure more of what you've worked for stays in your family's hands.

Let's start with a cautionary tale about the Johnsons. George and Elaine Johnson, a couple who owned a family farm that had been in their family for generations, were hit with a massive estate tax bill when George passed away. The bill was more than they could afford without selling part of the farm, leading to a loss of not just land but also the sense of connection they had to their legacy. This story underscores the importance of planning ahead to avoid such heartache and financial strain.

So, let's talk about estate taxes, what they are, and—most importantly—how you can minimize them to keep your legacy intact.

What Are Estate and Inheritance Taxes?

Estate and inheritance taxes, while not something most of us think about until they're staring us in the face, are crucial to understand. Even if they seem complicated at first, grasping these concepts is essential for effective estate planning.

Estate Taxes

Estate taxes, charged on the total value of your assets at the time of your death, are a significant consideration in estate planning. If the total value of your estate exceeds a certain threshold—$13.61 million per person as of 2024—the federal government takes a percentage of the amount over that threshold, often at rates between 18% and 40%.

Here's the good news: Most people won't hit that threshold. But for those who do—or those who live in states with lower estate tax thresholds—planning is essential.

Inheritance Taxes

Now, inheritance taxes are different. These are levied on the people who inherit your assets and are handled at the state level. The rate depends on the state and the relationship between the deceased and the heir. Spouses are usually exempt, but other beneficiaries, like nieces or friends, might pay anywhere from 1% to 18%.

If you're scratching your head right now, wondering whether you'd face estate or inheritance taxes, don't worry. We'll walk through how to figure it out and, more importantly, how to reduce or avoid them.

How Estate Taxes Work

Imagine you own a business worth $15 million. The federal estate tax threshold is $13.61 million. That means $1.39 million of your estate would be taxable. At a 40% tax rate, your heirs would owe $556,000. That's a hefty bill—and it's why people like George and Elaine end up losing part of their family legacy.

But here's the thing: you can avoid a situation like this with the right strategies. Let's examine how.

Strategies for Reducing Estate Taxes

Estate planning isn't about finding loopholes; it's about using innovative strategies to protect what matters most to you. It's about empowerment and taking control of your financial future.

Gifting Assets During Your Lifetime

One of the simplest ways to reduce your taxable estate is by giving away assets while you're still alive. The IRS lets you gift up to $18,000 per person per year (as of 2023) without paying gift taxes. Over time, these gifts can add up and significantly reduce the size of your estate.

Let me share an example. Carol and Jim had three kids and six grandkids. Every year, they gave each of them $18,000. That's $162,000 annually moved out of their estate—completely tax-free. Over ten years, they reduced their estate by more than $1.62 million, saving their heirs hundreds of thousands in estate taxes.

Using Trusts

Trusts are powerful tools for minimizing taxes and ensuring your assets are distributed according to your wishes.

- **Bypass Trusts**: Let's say you're married. A bypass trust allows you and your spouse to maximize your combined estate tax exemptions. When one spouse dies, part of their estate goes into the trust for the benefit of the surviving spouse and, eventually, the heirs. This keeps the assets out of the surviving spouse's taxable estate.

- **Charitable Remainder Trusts (CRTs)**: If giving back is important to you, a CRT lets you donate assets to charity while still receiving income from them during your lifetime. Not only does this reduce your taxable estate, but it also allows you to support causes you care about.

- **Grantor Retained Annuity Trusts (GRATs)**: These are

great for transferring appreciating assets to your beneficiaries. You place the asset in the trust, and the appreciation is passed on tax-free.

The Step-Up in Basis

Here's a perk that often gets overlooked. When your heirs inherit assets like stocks or real estate, they're usually valued at their fair market value on the date of your death. This "step-up in basis" reduces capital gains taxes when the assets are sold.

For example, if you bought a property for $200,000 and it's worth $500,000 when you pass away, your heirs won't pay taxes on the $300,000 gain. Instead, the property's new value becomes $500,000, and taxes are only owed on gains above that amount.

Real-Life Benefits: The Johnsons' Story

The Johnson family owned a small manufacturing business worth $15 million. Without planning, their children would've faced a massive tax bill—nearly $1 million—forcing them to sell part of the business. But the Johnsons worked with an estate planner to implement a strategy:

- They set up a bypass trust to maximize their exemptions.

- They gifted shares of the business to their children over time.

- They donated a portion of the business to charity through a

CRT.

The Result: The Johnsons reduced their taxable estate by $6 million, preserved the business, and left a meaningful gift to charity. Their children inherited the business without financial strain, and the family's legacy was intact.

Common Mistakes to Avoid

Even with the best intentions, mistakes can derail your estate plan. But by being aware of these common pitfalls, you can navigate your estate planning journey with confidence and security.

Procrastination

The earlier you start planning, the more options you have. Waiting until it's too late limits your ability to implement effective strategies.

Overlooking State Taxes

Many people focus on federal thresholds and must remember about state-level taxes, which can apply at much lower values.

Failing to Update Your Plan

Tax laws change, and so does life. Regularly revisiting your estate plan ensures it stays aligned with your goals and current laws.

Actionable Steps

Here's how to get started:

1. **Talk to a Tax Professional**: Find out how estate and inheritance taxes might impact you and your heirs.

2. **Start Gifting**: Use the annual gift exclusion to move assets out of your estate while you're alive.

3. **Explore Trusts**: Discuss options like bypass or charitable remainder trusts with your estate planner.

By taking these steps, you're not just saving money—you're keeping your family from unnecessary stress and ensuring your legacy is protected. Estate taxes might seem daunting, but with the right plan, you can minimize their impact and leave behind what truly matters.

Chapter Twelve

Navigating Family Dynamics in Blended Families

Let's start with a story about Maria and Carlos Ramirez. Both had been through the heartbreak of divorce and when they found each other, they felt like they were getting a second chance at love. Together, they built a beautiful blended family—Carlos had two daughters from his first marriage, Maria had a son from hers, and they shared a young son, Max. While their family dynamic wasn't perfect, Maria and Carlos worked hard to make everyone feel loved and included.

When it came to estate planning, though, things got tricky. Carlos wanted to ensure Maria would be taken care of if he passed away first, but he also wanted to ensure his daughters inherited some of his assets. Maria, on the other hand, wanted her family property—a small ranch that had been in her family for generations—to go to her biological son, James. Both Maria and Carlos agreed they needed to set something aside for Max.

As they sat down with an estate planner, Carlos joked, "It's like we need to divide the pie four ways, but we only have one pie. How do we make sure everyone gets a fair slice?"

Maria and Carlos aren't alone in their struggles. Estate planning in blended families can feel like a high-stakes balancing act, where every decision has the potential to upset someone. But with careful planning, open communication, and regular reviews of your estate plan, it's possible to create a plan that reflects your wishes while also honoring the dynamics of your blended family.

Why Blended Families Face Unique Challenges

Blended families, with their unique blend of love and complexity, are a beautiful tapestry of relationships. Whether you've remarried, have children from previous relationships, or are helping to raise stepchildren, the dynamics can be emotionally charged—especially when it comes to money and inheritance.

The Emotional Dynamics

One of the biggest challenges is balancing the needs and expectations of biological and stepchildren. Take Sarah and James, for example. When their father remarried, they assumed they'd still inherit the family home where they grew up. But after his passing, they discovered their stepmother, Laura, was the sole beneficiary. Sarah and James felt betrayed, not only by the estate plan but by the memory of their father. Meanwhile, Laura, who had cared for their father in his final years, felt unappreciated and misunderstood.

This kind of emotional fallout isn't uncommon. Children may fear being replaced or overlooked, while surviving spouses may feel pressured to prioritize their stepchildren over their own needs.

Avoiding Unintentional Disinheritance

Here's the harsh reality: without proper planning, it's possible to disinherit your biological children or stepchildren accidentally. Let me explain.

When someone passes away, their assets often go directly to their surviving spouse unless otherwise specified. This means that if a parent remarries and leaves everything to their new spouse, that spouse has complete control over the estate. While some spouses might honor informal promises to share the inheritance with stepchildren, there's no legal obligation for them to do so.

This is precisely what happened to Tim. After his father remarried, he assumed he'd still inherit part of his father's savings. But when his stepmother inherited everything, she decided to leave the money to her biological children instead. Tim was left with nothing—not because his father didn't care about him, but because his father hadn't put his wishes in writing.

How Trusts Can Help

If you're part of a blended family, trusts are one of the best tools for ensuring your estate is distributed fairly. Trusts allow you to specify exactly how your assets will be managed and who will benefit from them, making them ideal for complex family dynamics.

Revocable Living Trusts

A revocable living trust lets you maintain control over your assets during your lifetime while ensuring a smooth transfer after your death. This type of trust can be updated as family circumstances change, making it a flexible option for blended families.

For example, Maria and Carlos used a revocable living trust to divide their shared assets equally among all their children. This gave them peace of mind, knowing their estate plan would adapt if their family's needs changed.

QTIP Trusts

A Qualified Terminable Interest Property (QTIP) trust is designed to balance the needs of a surviving spouse with the inheritance of biological children. Here's how it works: the trust provides income to the surviving spouse for their lifetime, but the principal is preserved for the children.

Carlos decided to use a QTIP trust to ensure Maria could live comfortably if he passed away first while guaranteeing his daughters would inherit a portion of his estate. "This way," he told Maria, "everyone gets what they need without feeling left out."

Separate Trusts for Biological and Stepchildren

In some cases, it makes sense to create separate trusts for different groups of beneficiaries. For example, Maria set up a trust specifically for James to inherit her family ranch, ensuring it stayed within her biological family while also contributing to the shared trust for Max.

The Power of Clear Documentation

One of the simplest ways to avoid conflict is to document your wishes. When everyone knows exactly how assets will be distributed—and why—it reduces the potential for misunderstandings and resentment, fostering a more harmonious family dynamic.

Wills and Trusts

A will outlines your general intentions, but trusts provide more control over how and when assets are distributed. For blended families, using both tools together creates a comprehensive plan.

Beneficiary Designations

It's not enough to have a will. You must also update beneficiary designations on life insurance, retirement funds, and payable-on-death accounts. Outdated designations can override your will, creating confusion and frustration.

The Importance of Communication

Let me tell you about the Carters. When John and Linda remarried, they sat their children down for a family meeting to discuss their estate plan. John explained that Linda would receive a portion of his estate, but the rest would go into a trust for his biological children. Linda shared her plan to leave specific assets to her stepchildren while ensuring her biological children inherited her home.

At first, the conversation was awkward. The children had questions—some even voiced concerns. But by the end of the meeting, everyone felt included and informed. "It wasn't easy," Linda admitted later, "but it was worth it. We wanted everyone to feel valued."

Family meetings like this can prevent misunderstandings and ensure everyone understands the reasoning behind your decisions. And if a meeting feels too formal, you can always write a legacy letter—a heartfelt explanation of your choices.

Preventing and Resolving Conflicts

Even with the best intentions, conflicts can arise. The key is to address potential issues proactively.

Balancing Financial and Emotional Needs

Sometimes, "fair" doesn't mean "equal." For example, if one child has greater financial needs, it's okay to allocate more resources to them while providing sentimental items or smaller shares to others. The important thing is to explain your reasoning.

Using Neutral Executors

To avoid accusations of favoritism, consider appointing a neutral third party—like a professional fiduciary or attorney—as the executor of your estate.

Regularly Reviewing Your Plan

Life changes, and so should your estate plan. Significant events like remarriage, the birth of a grandchild, or a child's marriage are good reasons to revisit and update your plan.

The Ramirez Family: A Success Story

Let's revisit Maria and Carlos. After working with their estate planner, they created a plan that reflected their family's unique dynamics:

- They used a QTIP trust to ensure Maria would be cared for if Carlos passed first while preserving assets for his daughters.

- Maria created a separate trust for her son, James, to inherit her family ranch.

- Together, they held a family meeting to explain their decisions, allowing each child to ask questions and share their feelings.

When Carlos eventually passed away, the plan worked seamlessly. Maria felt secure knowing she was provided for, and Carlos's daughters were grateful their father had thought of them. The family continued to gather at the ranch for holidays, honoring both Maria's and Carlos's legacies.

Actionable Steps

Here's how you can take action today:

1. **Evaluate Your Current Plan**:

    - Does it address the needs of your biological children, stepchildren, and spouse?

2. **Consult an Estate Planner**:

    - Work with a professional to explore options like trusts and wills.

3. **Communicate with Your Family**:

    - Hold a family meeting or write a legacy letter to share your intentions.

Blended families may have unique challenges, but with thoughtful planning and open communication, you can create an estate plan that reflects your love for everyone involved. By taking these steps, you're not just dividing assets—you're building a legacy of fairness and understanding.

Chapter Thirteen

Regularly Reviewing and Updating Your Plan

Let me tell you about the Taylor family. When Jim and Laura Taylor first created their estate plan, their kids were teenagers, and life was relatively simple. Their primary concerns were naming a guardian for their children and ensuring their modest home and savings would be passed on smoothly if something happened to them. Fast-forward 15 years: their children were grown, Jim had started a small business, and their daughter had recently married.

It wasn't until their daughter's divorce five years later that the Taylors realized their estate plan had been stuck in the past. An outdated beneficiary designation meant their ex-son-in-law still stood to inherit partial ownership of Jim's business if something happened to them. "It never even crossed our minds," Laura admitted. "We thought we'd taken care of everything years ago."

The Taylors' story reminds us that estate planning isn't a one-and-done task. Your life and family change and your estate plan needs to change with them. Regularly reviewing and updating your plan ensures it reflects your current reality and protects the people you love most.

Why Updating Your Plan Matters

Your estate plan is like a snapshot of your life at a particular moment. But life is a moving picture, not a still photo. A plan that made sense five or ten years ago might not work today. Failure to update it can be costly—not just financially but emotionally.

Preventing Unintended Outcomes

One of the most common mistakes people make is assuming their estate plan will naturally adjust to life changes. Unfortunately, that's not how it works. Outdated plans can lead to unintended consequences, like an ex-spouse inheriting assets, new family members being excluded, or heirs facing unnecessary taxes.

For example, imagine you named your sibling as the guardian for your minor children when they were first born. Fifteen years later, your sibling has moved across the country and isn't as close to your family anymore. If you never updated your will, your children could end up in a situation that doesn't align with your current wishes.

When to Review Your Plan

So, when should you review your estate plan? The short answer is anytime your life changes significantly.

Major Life Events

- **Marriage or Divorce**: Adding a new spouse or parting ways with one changes everything. You'll need to update beneficiary designations, adjust inheritance plans, and potentially revise trusts or wills.

- **Birth or Adoption of a Child**: New additions to the family are a big reason to revisit your plan. You'll want to ensure your new child or grandchild is included as a beneficiary and assign guardianship for minors.

- **Death of a Loved One**: If someone named in your estate plan passes away, you'll need to update roles like executor or trustee and reconsider how assets are distributed.

- **Health Changes**: A serious illness or disability might prompt changes to your healthcare directives or provisions for long-term care.

Financial Changes

- **Increase in Wealth**: Whether it's a new job, an inheritance, or a successful investment, significant financial changes require you to revisit your plan to minimize taxes and ensure proper distribution.

- **Loss of Assets**: If you sell a property, close an account, or lose value in an investment, you'll need to adjust your plan to reflect your current resources.

Legislative Changes

Estate tax laws and regulations are constantly evolving. For example, the federal estate tax exemption changes periodically, and some states impose their own inheritance taxes. A review ensures your plan takes advantage of the latest tax-saving opportunities.

What to Review

When reviewing your estate plan, it helps to have a checklist of what to focus on.

Beneficiary Designations

One of the most overlooked areas in estate planning is updating beneficiary designations on accounts like life insurance, retirement funds, and payable-on-death accounts. These designations override your will, so if they're outdated, your assets might not go where you intended.

Example: A man divorced his first wife but forgot to update his life insurance policy beneficiary. When he passed away, his ex-wife received the payout instead of his current spouse.

Asset Inventory

Life moves fast, and it's easy to forget to add new assets—or remove old ones—from your estate plan. Ensure your list of assets is up-to-date, including properties, investments, digital accounts, and sentimental items like family heirlooms.

Wills and Trusts

Review the terms of your will and any trusts you've created. Do they still reflect your wishes? Are the appointed guardians, trustees, or executors still the right people for the job?

Healthcare Directives

Your healthcare proxy and living will should reflect your current medical preferences and designate someone you trust to make decisions if you are unable to.

Powers of Attorney

Check that the people you've named as your financial and healthcare powers of attorney are still capable and willing to act on your behalf.

The Importance of Professional Help

Reviewing your plan doesn't have to be a solo effort. In fact, working with professionals can help you spot issues you might not notice on your own, providing you with a sense of reassurance and peace of mind.

Estate Attorneys

An attorney ensures your plan is legally compliant and up-to-date with state and federal laws. They can also help you navigate complex situations, such as blended families or multi-state assets.

Financial Advisors

A financial advisor can help align your estate plan with your overall financial goals, ensuring your assets are distributed efficiently and tax-effectively.

Collaborative Approach

Encourage communication between your attorney, financial advisor, and accountant. A coordinated effort ensures every aspect of your plan works together seamlessly, empowering you to be in control of your estate planning journey.

Storytime: The Taylors' Lesson

Let's go back to the Taylors. After their daughter's divorce, Jim and Laura realized their estate plan hadn't kept up with their changing family dynamics. Their outdated plan still listed their ex-son-in-law as a beneficiary and left their son as the sole trustee of their family trust—a role he wasn't comfortable handling.

The Taylors met with their estate planner and worked through each part of their plan:

- They updated beneficiary designations to remove their ex-son-in-law and include their new granddaughter.

- They revised their will to divide assets equally among their children, including new provisions for their grandchildren's education.

- They named a professional fiduciary as trustee, relieving their son of a responsibility he didn't want.

When Jim passed away a few years later, the updated plan worked exactly as intended. "It was one of the best decisions we ever made," Laura said. "We avoided so many potential problems just by taking the time to review everything."

How Often to Review

There's no hard-and-fast rule, but here's a simple guideline:

- **Regular Reviews**: Set aside time annually or biannually to review your plan. Tie it to a consistent event, like tax season, to make it a habit.

- **As-Needed Reviews**: Revisit your plan whenever a significant life event occurs, such as a marriage, divorce, birth, death, or significant financial change.

Practical Checklist for Reviewing Your Plan

Here's a checklist to guide you through your next review:

1. **Update Beneficiaries**: Ensure all accounts have accurate, up-to-date beneficiaries.

2. **Inventory Your Assets**: Add any new assets and remove those you no longer own.

3. **Evaluate Guardianship Provisions**: Confirm that the named guardians for minor children or dependents are still appropriate.

4. **Review Tax Strategies**: Check that your plan reflects current tax laws and minimizes potential tax burdens.

5. **Confirm Healthcare Directives**: Ensure medical proxies and living will align with your preferences.

Actionable Steps

To get started, here's what you can do today:

1. Schedule an annual or biannual date to review your estate plan. Pick a day that's easy to remember, like your birthday

or tax season.

2. Consult with an estate attorney and financial advisor to make sure your plan is comprehensive and legally sound.

3. Share updates with your family or key stakeholders to ensure everyone is on the same page.

Closing Thoughts

Your estate plan is one of the most important ways you protect your loved ones and preserve your legacy. By reviewing and updating it regularly, you're not just planning for the future—you're ensuring peace of mind for everyone involved.

Chapter Fourteen

Legacy Planning—Building Meaning That Lasts

When Evelyn started thinking about her estate plan, she realized she wanted to leave more than just money behind. She had worked hard, saved diligently, and had a comfortable nest egg. Still, she wanted to pass on her passion for education. As a retired teacher, Evelyn believed that education was the great equalizer—the key to opportunity and a better life. "What good is leaving money if it doesn't reflect who I am or what I stand for?" she often said.

With her estate planner's guidance, Evelyn created a scholarship fund for underserved students in her community. But she didn't stop there. She wrote heartfelt letters to each of her grandchildren, sharing life lessons and stories from her own childhood. She even worked with her daughter to compile a family recipe book, complete with notes about where each dish had come from and the memories tied to them. "I want them to remember me for more than just what I left behind," Evelyn said. And they did. The emotional fulfillment she experienced from these acts of legacy was immeasurable, inspiring her and those around her.

Evelyn's story is a reminder that your legacy is so much more than dollars and cents. It's the values you've lived by, the traditions you've cherished, and the impact you've made on others. Estate planning isn't just about dividing assets—it's about shaping the mark you leave on the world. It's about creating a personal connection that transcends generations, making your presence felt even when you're no longer here.

What Does Legacy Mean to You?

When most people think of a legacy, they immediately think of wealth—money, property, or heirlooms passed down to the next generation. But a true legacy goes much deeper than that. It's the values you've lived by, the stories you've told, and the impact you've made on others.

Think about it. What do you want your loved ones to remember about you? Maybe it's the way you always volunteered at the local food bank or how you turned family dinners into a nightly ritual of storytelling and laughter. Maybe it's the way you worked hard to put your kids through college or your passion for preserving the environment. These are the things that define you, and they're what your legacy should reflect.

Legacy planning starts with asking yourself one simple question: What do I want to be remembered for?

Preserving Your Family's History

Let me tell you about Jack. Jack was an immigrant who came to the United States with little more than a suitcase and a dream. He worked long hours, saved every penny, and eventually built a small but thriving business. But for Jack, his greatest pride wasn't in what he'd built—it was in the lessons he'd learned along the way.

When Jack sat down to work on his estate plan, his attorney suggested he write a family history. At first, Jack was skeptical. "Who's going to want to read about an old man's life?" he asked. But with a bit of encouragement, he started writing. He described his journey to America, the hardships he faced, and the values that guided him—hard work, honesty, and gratitude. He even included stories about his childhood in Ireland, complete with colorful anecdotes about his mischievous brothers. These personal stories not only engaged his family but also connected them to their roots and to Jack.

When Jack passed away, his family discovered the memoir among his papers. It became a cherished family treasure, read aloud at reunions and shared with future generations. 'I never knew these stories about Grandpa,' one of his grandkids said. 'It makes me feel like I know him better, even though he's gone.' This emotional connection is a testament to the power of preserving family history.

Preserving your family's history doesn't have to be a daunting task. It can be as simple as jotting down a few favorite memories, creating a digital archive of family photos, or recording yourself telling stories from your life. These small acts can significantly impact your family, keeping them connected to its roots and to you.

Supporting Future Generations

Another powerful way to build your legacy is by supporting the people who come after you. For many, that means helping their children and grandchildren achieve their dreams.

Lisa and Tom knew they wanted to help their grandchildren go to college. "We worked hard so they wouldn't have to struggle the way we did," Lisa said. But instead of leaving a lump sum in their will, they decided to set up an education trust. This trust would cover tuition, books, and other expenses for any grandchild who wanted to pursue higher education. "It's not just about the money," Tom added. "It's about showing them that we believe in them and their future."

Education trusts are just one way to support future generations. Some families create funds to help with other goals, like starting a business or buying a first home. The key is to think about what matters most to you and how you can use your resources to make a lasting impact.

Making a Difference Through Philanthropy

Evelyn's scholarship fund wasn't just about her family—it was about her community. She wanted to give students the same opportunities she had worked hard to provide for her children. "It feels good to know I'm helping someone achieve their dreams," she said.

Philanthropy is a powerful way to extend your legacy beyond your immediate family. You can set up a charitable foundation, establish a donor-advised fund, or simply include charitable gifts in your will. The best part? It doesn't have to be complicated or require a fortune. Even small contributions can make a big difference when they're tied to something you care deeply about.

Take John, a retired doctor who loved the arts. He set aside a portion of his estate to support local theater programs in his town. "I spent my life helping people stay healthy," he said, "but art feeds the soul. This is my way of giving back to something that brought me so much joy."

Tying Your Legacy to Your Estate Plan

Your estate plan is more than just a legal document—it's the blueprint for your legacy. With the right tools and a little creativity, you can ensure your values and vision are carried forward.

Trusts are one of the most effective tools for legacy planning. Whether you're setting up an education trust for your grandchildren or a philanthropic trust to support a cause you care about, trusts give you control and flexibility. You can specify how and when funds are distributed, ensuring they're used in ways that align with your goals.

Another way to personalize your estate plan is by including letters or videos for your heirs. Imagine your grandchildren hearing your voice, reading your words, explaining why you made certain decisions, or sharing advice for the future. These personal touches can make your plan feel less like a legal document and more like a love letter to your family.

What Will Your Legacy Be?

Legacy planning isn't about being perfect or having all the answers. It's about reflecting on what matters most to you and finding ways to ensure those values live on.

Start small. Write down three things you want your legacy to reflect—maybe your love of learning, your commitment to family, or your passion for helping others. Then, think about how your estate plan can support those goals. Whether it's through a scholarship fund, a trust, or a simple letter, every action you take brings your legacy to life.

Closing Thoughts and Actionable Steps

When Evelyn's family gathered after her passing, they didn't just talk about the scholarship fund or the money she had left behind. They spoke of the letters she had written, the stories she had shared, and their memories of her. They celebrated her values, her impact, and the love she poured into her legacy.

That's the power of legacy planning. It's not just about dividing assets—it's about building meaning that lasts. And it starts with a single step: deciding what kind of legacy you want to leave.

Your Next Steps

1. **Reflect on Your Values**: Take a moment to write down three things you want to be remembered for. These might be values, traditions, or causes that are important to you.

2. **Choose One Legacy Project**: Whether it's creating a family archive, setting up a trust, or supporting a cause you care about, pick one way to begin building your legacy.

3. **Consult a Professional**: Meet with an estate planner or financial advisor to incorporate your legacy goals into your estate plan.

4. **Communicate Your Wishes**: Share your plans with your family. Whether through a conversation, a letter, or a video, let them know what matters most to you and why.

By taking these steps, you're not just planning for the future—you're creating a legacy that reflects the best parts of who you are and what you've stood for. Every action you take today brings that legacy closer to reality.

Chapter Fifteen

Ensuring Peace of Mind Through Comprehensive Planning

When Susan and Robert Johnson first sat down to discuss their estate plan, they felt overwhelmed. "It's not just about the money," Susan said. "It's about making sure our family is cared for and that we leave behind something meaningful." Robert nodded, adding, "But how do we make it all fit together? There are many moving pieces—our kids, business, the house, even the old vacation cabin."

Their estate planner smiled. "That's what we're here to figure out. A good estate plan isn't just a collection of documents—it's a cohesive strategy that reflects your values, protects your loved ones, and gives you peace of mind."

By the end of their planning process, Susan and Robert had more than just a binder of paperwork. They had a plan that preserved their family's financial security, honored their shared love for philanthropy, and ensured their children understood the legacy they wanted to leave behind. "It's like a weight has been lifted," Susan said. "We know we've done everything we can to take care of the people we love." This sense of relief and peace of mind is a common outcome of a well-crafted estate plan.

Their story shows how comprehensive planning brings together all the pieces of your estate—financial, emotional, and personal—into a harmonious whole. Let's explore what that means and how you can achieve it.

Why a Holistic Plan Matters

An estate plan isn't just about deciding who gets what. It's about creating a roadmap that covers every aspect of your life, from financial assets to healthcare decisions, digital accounts, and personal legacies. Gaps can lead to confusion, conflict, or even unintended consequences without a comprehensive approach.

Take Lisa, for example. Lisa thought her simple will was enough to handle her estate. But when she passed, her family discovered she hadn't updated her life insurance beneficiary after her divorce. Her ex-husband received the payout instead of her children simply because she hadn't coordinated her plan's elements. It was a painful and expensive lesson for her family—and one that could have been avoided.

A holistic plan ties everything together, ensuring no detail is overlooked.

The Building Blocks of a Comprehensive Plan

Let's start with the basics. A strong estate plan typically includes several key components:

Wills and Trusts

These are the backbone of your estate plan. A will ensures your assets are distributed according to your wishes, while trusts offer more control and flexibility, such as avoiding probate or providing for minor children. For families with complex dynamics, trusts can balance competing interests—like supporting a surviving spouse while preserving assets for children from a previous marriage.

Healthcare Directives

Your healthcare directives outline your medical wishes if you're unable to make decisions for yourself. This includes a living will specifying the type of care you want and a healthcare proxy, which names someone to act on your behalf. These documents spare your family from the emotional burden of guessing what you would want.

Powers of Attorney

A power of attorney allows a trusted person to manage your financial affairs if you're incapacitated. Without one, your family might face legal hurdles to access your accounts or pay your bills.

Digital Assets

In today's world, your estate plan isn't complete without addressing digital assets. This includes everything from online banking and cryptocurrency to social media accounts and photos stored in the cloud. Designating a digital executor can simplify this often-overlooked aspect of planning.

Legacy Beyond Finances

Your estate isn't just about assets; it's also about the values, traditions, and stories that define your life. Incorporating these elements into your plan adds depth and meaning.

Passing Down Values

The Johnsons wanted their plan to reflect their commitment to giving back. They set up a charitable trust to support local education initiatives, a cause they had championed throughout their lives. "We wanted our kids to see that it's not just about what you take—it's about what you give," Robert said.

Preserving Family Traditions

Some families allocate resources to continue beloved traditions, like annual reunions or holiday celebrations. For the Johnsons, this meant setting aside a small fund to maintain the family's vacation cabin, where their children and grandchildren had built countless memories.

Storytelling and Personal Messages

Including letters or videos in your estate plan can offer personal insights that go beyond financial decisions. Imagine your loved ones hearing your voice or reading your words, explaining the reasons behind your choices, or sharing life lessons. It's a powerful way to stay connected even after you're gone.

The Psychological Benefits of Planning

Let's not underestimate the emotional impact of having a plan in place. A well-crafted estate plan isn't just practical—it's profoundly reassuring.

Peace of Mind

Knowing your loved ones will be cared for and your wishes honored brings a sense of calm. "I can finally sleep at night," Susan said after completing her plan. "I know my family won't have to worry."

Easing the Burden on Loved Ones

A clear and comprehensive plan prevents misunderstandings and reduces the stress on your family during an already difficult time. It also minimizes the chances of disputes, which can strain relationships.

Strengthening Family Bonds

The Johnsons discovered that working on their estate plan together was an opportunity to connect as a family. "It wasn't just about the money," Susan said. "It was about talking openly about what matters to us and how we want to be remembered."

How to Get Started

Creating a comprehensive estate plan might feel overwhelming, but breaking it down into steps makes the process manageable.

Reflect on Your Goals

Ask yourself what you want your estate plan to achieve. Is it about providing for your family, supporting a cause, preserving a tradition, or something else? Your answers will shape your strategy.

Work with Professionals

An estate attorney, financial advisor, and accountant can help craft a legally sound, tax-efficient plan aligned with your goals. Their expertise and guidance are invaluable in creating a plan that reflects your vision and ensures your legacy is preserved.

Communicate with Your Family

Sharing your plan with loved ones ensures they understand your wishes and reduces the likelihood of misunderstandings. Consider holding a family meeting to explain your decisions and invite input.

Review and Update Regularly

Life changes and your estate plan should change with it. Whether it's a marriage, a new grandchild, or a shift in financial circumstances, revisiting your plan ensures it stays relevant. This proactive approach to planning gives you the control to adapt your plan to your evolving life.

Storytime: How the Johnsons Found Peace

When Susan and Robert Johnson finalized their estate plan, they didn't just feel a sense of accomplishment—they felt closer as a family. The process of discussing their values and priorities brought clarity and connection, turning what initially felt like a daunting task into a meaningful journey. Their children, too, appreciated the openness. "It's comforting to know what Mom and Dad want," their daughter said. "There's no guessing, no tension—just a plan that reflects who they are."

Your Next Steps

1. **Reflect on Your Legacy**: Write down three ways you want your estate plan to reflect your values, traditions, or goals.

2. **Consult Professionals**: Schedule a meeting with an estate planner, financial advisor, or attorney to start crafting or refining your plan.

3. **Share Your Vision**: Talk to your family about your wishes and invite them into the conversation.

4. **Set a Review Schedule**: Commit to revisiting your plan annually or after major life changes to keep it up-to-date.

A comprehensive estate plan is more than a legal safeguard—it's a gift to your family and a reflection of your life's purpose. Planning thoughtfully ensures peace of mind for yourself and those you love, leaving behind assets and a legacy of care, connection, and meaning.

Chapter Sixteen

Conclusion: Taking the First Step

When Evelyn finalized her estate plan, she said something that stuck with me: "It's not just about what I'm leaving behind—it's about how I'm leaving it." Evelyn had taken the time to think deeply about her family, values, and impact on the world. Her estate plan wasn't just a collection of documents but a reflection of who she was and what she stood for. And in doing so, she gave her family the greatest gift of all—clarity, security, and peace of mind.

As you close this book, I hope you feel a profound sense of empowerment. You've taken the time to learn about estate planning, and that's a monumental first step. But remember, knowledge alone isn't enough. It's what you do with it that matters. The stories, strategies, and advice you've read are tools to help you take action, starting today.

A Quick Recap: What You've Learned

Over the course of this book, we've explored what it means to create a comprehensive, meaningful estate plan. Let's quickly revisit the key lessons:

- **Start Early**: Estate planning isn't something to put off until "someday." The earlier you start, the more options you have and the more prepared you'll be for life's uncertainties.

- **Update Often**: Life changes—marriages, divorces, births, deaths, new jobs, new homes. Your estate plan should evolve alongside these changes to stay relevant.

- **Think Holistically**: Estate planning goes beyond dividing assets. It's about protecting your family, honoring your values, and leaving a legacy reflecting your identity.

Why You Should Act Now

I get it—estate planning can feel overwhelming. Maybe you're unsure where to start or afraid of making the wrong decision. Maybe you've told yourself there's still plenty of time. But here's the truth: the best time to start was yesterday. The second-best time is today.

Consider the peace of mind that comes with knowing your family is cared for. Consider the sense of accomplishment you'll feel when you've taken control of your future. And most importantly, consider the relief your loved ones will experience when your wishes are clearly laid out, sparing them from confusion or conflict. This is a responsibility we all carry, and it's one we should take seriously.

The most important thing is to start. You don't have to do everything at once. Estate planning is a process; even small steps can lead to big results. The key is to start, to take that first step. Once you do, you'll find that the rest of the journey becomes clearer and more manageable.

Your First Steps

Right now, while the ideas are fresh in your mind, I want you to make a commitment. Think back to the actionable steps in this book. Which one spoke to you the most? Was it creating a digital asset inventory? Setting up a trust? Writing a letter to your family?

Choose one step—just one—and commit to completing it this week. Maybe it's as simple as scheduling a meeting with an estate planner or updating your beneficiary designations. Whatever it is, make it a priority. That first step is the hardest but also the most important.

If you need guidance, remember that you're not alone. This book's companion website is a valuable resource that includes tools, checklists, and templates to help you get started and navigate the complexities of estate planning. Use the QR code in the book to access these resources and take the next step toward securing your family's future.

Final Thoughts

Estate planning isn't just a task to check off your to-do list. It's an opportunity to reflect on what matters most to you—your family, your values, your legacy—and make decisions to protect and honor those priorities. It's about more than dividing assets; it's about leaving a mark on the world and the people you love.

By finishing this book, you've already taken an enormous step forward. You've invested time and effort into understanding what it takes to build a thoughtful, comprehensive estate plan. And for that, I want to thank you. Your dedication to this process shows how much you care about your loved ones and your legacy.

Now it's time to act. Your journey is just beginning, and every action you take brings you closer to the peace of mind that comes with knowing your affairs are in order. Remember: every great journey starts with a single step, and you've already taken yours.

Your Commitment

Before you set this book down, I urge you to make a promise to yourself: Choose one action item from these pages and take the first step today. Your future self—and your loved ones—will thank you. Your commitment to this process is crucial, and I believe in your ability to make a difference in your family's future.

Keeping the Legacy Alive

Now that you have everything you need to create an estate plan that protects your loved ones and preserves your legacy, it's time to pay it forward.

By sharing your honest thoughts about this book on Amazon, you'll help others who are searching for simple, straightforward advice about estate planning. Your review can guide them to the tools and information they need to secure their future and protect the people they care about most.

Your feedback doesn't just help others—it helps keep the mission of empowering families and simplifying estate planning alive.

Thank you for your support. The knowledge and confidence we share with one another create a lasting impact, and you're helping to make that possible.

Together, we're ensuring that estate planning becomes easier, more approachable, and accessible to everyone.

To share your thoughts and leave your review, simply scan the QR code or visit this link:

https://www.amazon.com/review/review-your-purchases/?asin=B0DPVVLGHH

Thank you for helping others take the next step in protecting their legacy.

Jeff Kikel

p.s. Don't forget to go to our resource page for the book to download your FREE worksheets and guides and get a 10% discount at Trust & Will.

Scan me

https://www.surehorizonretirement.com/estate-planning-essentials

Glossary

Advance Directive (Living Will)
A legal document outlining your medical treatment preferences if you're unable to communicate. It includes choices about life support, resuscitation, and other critical healthcare decisions.

Beneficiary
An individual or entity designated to receive assets from your estate, life insurance, or retirement accounts upon your death.

Charitable Trust
A trust established to provide financial support to charities while offering tax benefits to the donor.

Digital Assets
Online accounts and digital property such as social media profiles, email accounts, cryptocurrency wallets, and cloud storage files. These assets often require a digital executor for proper management after death.

Digital Executor
A person designated to manage digital assets according to your wishes after your death.

Durable Power of Attorney

A legal document that allows someone you trust to handle your financial affairs if you become incapacitated.

Estate

The total of all assets you own at the time of your death, including real estate, financial accounts, personal belongings, and digital assets.

Estate Planning

The process of arranging the management and distribution of your assets after death or in case of incapacity. It often includes wills, trusts, powers of attorney, and healthcare directives.

Executor

The person responsible for carrying out the instructions in your will, such as distributing assets and settling debts.

Gift Tax

A federal tax on transfers of money or property made as a gift above a specified annual exemption amount.

Guardian

An individual appointed in a will to care for minor children or dependents in the event of your death.

Healthcare Directive (Living Will)
See **Advance Directive**.

Healthcare Proxy (Medical Power of Attorney)
A legal document naming someone to make healthcare decisions on your behalf if you are unable to do so.

Intestate
The state of dying without a will. In this case, state laws determine how your assets are distributed.

Irrevocable Trust
A trust that cannot be altered, modified, or revoked after it is created. It is often used for tax savings and asset protection.

Joint Tenancy with Right of Survivorship (JTWROS)
A form of property ownership in which two or more people share equal ownership, and the surviving owner(s) automatically inherit the deceased's share.

Last Will and Testament
A legal document that outlines how your assets should be distributed and names guardians for any minor children.

Living Trust (Revocable Trust)
A trust created during a person's lifetime to manage assets. It can be modified or revoked and helps avoid probate.

Medical Power of Attorney
See **Healthcare Proxy**.

Payable-on-Death (POD) Account
A bank account that passes directly to the named beneficiary upon the account holder's death, avoiding probate.

Pet Trust
A legal arrangement ensuring the care of pets after your death, often including funds for their care.

Power of Attorney (POA)
A legal document granting someone the authority to act on your behalf for financial, legal, or medical matters.

Probate
The legal process of validating a will, settling debts, and distributing assets. It can be time-consuming and expensive.

Special Needs Trust
A trust designed to provide for a beneficiary with disabilities without affecting their eligibility for government benefits.

Testamentary Trust
A trust established through a will, which takes effect after the death of the individual.

Transfer-on-Death (TOD) Designation
A designation on financial accounts or real estate that transfers ownership directly to a named beneficiary upon the owner's death.

Trust

A legal arrangement where one party (the trustee) holds and manages assets for the benefit of another (the beneficiary).

Trustee

The person or entity responsible for managing and distributing the assets in a trust according to its terms.

Will

See **Last Will and Testament**.

Index

A

- Advance Directive (Living Will): 8, 45, 82, 117
- Asset Inventory: 12, 50, 78
- Attorney: choosing the right one, 15, 43, 66
- Asset Titling: significance in estate planning, 32, 40

B

- Beneficiary Designations:
  - Importance of updating, 14, 46, 112
  - Errors to avoid, 35
- Blended Families: estate planning strategies, 59, 89

C

- Charitable Giving:

- Establishing a trust, 90, 109
- Tax benefits, 72, 94

- Communication:
  - Discussing plans with family, 14, 42
  - Avoiding misunderstandings, 64, 80

D

- Digital Assets:
  - Managing and inventorying, 33, 51, 99
  - Designating a digital executor, 34, 58
- Durable Power of Attorney: 26, 45, 80

E

- Estate Planning Basics: 2, 6, 12
- Executor:
  - Roles and responsibilities, 22, 43, 68
  - Choosing the right person, 44

F

- Family Meetings:
  - Importance in estate planning, 42, 76
- Financial Advisors:
  - Collaborating with attorneys, 12, 40, 67

G

- Guardianship: appointing for minors, 25, 47

H

- Healthcare Directives:
  - Documenting preferences, 8, 46
  - Appointing a healthcare proxy, 45

I

- Intestate Succession: 19, 28

L

- Legacy Planning:

- Creating personal impact, 91, 109
- Philanthropy, 94

M

- Medical Power of Attorney: 24, 47
- Minor Children: planning for, 25, 47

P

- Probate:
  - Definition and process, 18, 40
  - How to avoid, 22, 38
- Philanthropic Planning: 92

R

- Revocable Trusts:
  - Benefits and flexibility, 28, 44, 82

T

- Taxes:

- Minimizing through estate planning, 20, 46, 71
- Trusts:
  - Different types, 25, 35, 60
  - Setting up, 36

W

- Wills:
  - Creating and reviewing, 16, 24
  - Common mistakes, 30

Other Books By Jeff Kikel

Sure Horizon Retirement Series (Available on Amazon.com or www.SureHorizonRetirement.com)

1. **10 Critical Mistakes in Retirement Planning (and How to Fix Them): A Practical Guide to Securing Your Financial Freedom and Retirement Income**
   Discover the most common retirement planning mistakes and how to avoid them with clear strategies and easy-to-follow steps.

2. **The Retirement Income Equation: Proven Strategies for Secure, Flexible, and Prosperous Retirement**
   Learn how to build a reliable retirement income plan that balances security and flexibility for a worry-free future.

3. **Identity Theft: The Road to Recovery: How to Protect Yourself as a Retiree, Avoid Becoming a Victim, and Recover From Identity Theft**
   Protect yourself from identity theft with this essential guide,

featuring preventive measures and recovery strategies tailored for retirees.

4. **Social Security Essentials: How to Understand the Basics, Decide When to File, and Maximize Benefits Over Your Life**
Demystify Social Security with a step-by-step guide to understanding your options, filing strategies, and maximizing benefits.

5. **Medicare Essentials: Easily Navigate Medicare Insurance, Avoid Costly Pitfalls, and Secure Financial Peace of Mind with the Best Coverage**
Navigate the complexities of Medicare with confidence and avoid common mistakes with this comprehensive resource.

6. **Long-Term Care Essentials: A Practical Guide to Long-Term Care Planning, Financial Protection, and Caring for Aging Parents**
Plan for your long-term care needs and protect your family's future with this empathetic and practical guide.

7. **Estate Planning Essentials: A Comprehensive Guide to Preserving Your Estate, Minimizing Probate and Taxes, and Ensuring Your Legacy**
Secure your family's future with this approachable and thorough guide to estate planning. Learn how to preserve your legacy and ensure your wishes are carried out.

Coming Soon

Jeff continues to expand the *Sure Horizon Retirement Series* with upcoming titles, including:

- **Building a Tax-Free Retirement**

- **Life After Retirement: Designing a Retired Life That is Fulfilling, Rewarding, and Fun**

Stay tuned for more practical and empowering resources to guide you through every stage of retirement.

Freedom Day Series (Available at www.FFreedomDay Method.com or Amazon.com)

1. **Overcoming the** Retirement Trap: An 8-Step Financial Freedom Blueprint For Your Journey To Building Wealth, Creating Financial Independence, and Living A Life Beyond Limits

Family Finance Series (Available at www.YourFamilyYourFinances.com or Amazon.com)

1. Family Financial Playbook

About The Author

Jeff Kikel

Jeff Kikel is a seasoned financial expert with over two decades of experience helping individuals and families secure their financial futures. As the founder of **Sure Horizon Retirement**, Jeff is dedicated to making the complexities of retirement planning simple and approachable for everyone. His passion is helping people navigate the often-confusing world of **Medicare, Social Security**, Estate Planning, and other essential aspects of retirement.

Jeff's straightforward, no-nonsense approach has helped thousands of retirees make informed decisions about their healthcare and finances, empowering them to live the retirement they've always dreamed of. Through his **Sure Horizon Retirement Series**, Jeff shares practical advice, real-life strategies, and his signature conversational style to guide readers through retirement planning.

When Jeff isn't helping others achieve financial peace of mind, he enjoys spending time with his family, traveling, and exploring the great outdoors. He believes retirement should be the best years of your life, and his mission is to make that possible for as many people as possible.

Jeff currently lives in Cedar Park, TX, with his wife and business partner, Crystal. He continues expanding his book series to cover all aspects of retirement planning.